'don't ask for stories . . .'

THE WOMEN FROM ERNABELLA AND THEIR ART

'tjukurpa tjapintja wiya . . .'

MINYMA ANAPALANYA NGURARA TJUTANGKU WARKA PALYANTJA CRAFTROOMANGKA

Readers of this work should be aware that in some Aboriginal communities, seeing the names and photographs of the deceased may cause sadness and distress, particularly to relatives of those people. Before using this work in such communities, readers should establish the wishes of senior community members and take their advice on any procedures and safeguards to be adopted.

‘don’t ask for stories . . .’

THE WOMEN FROM ERNABELLA AND THEIR ART

‘tjukurpa tjapintja wiya . . .’

MINYMA ANAPALANYA NGURARA TJUTANGKU WARKA PALYANTJA CRAFTROOMANGKA

Compiled by Ute Eickelkamp

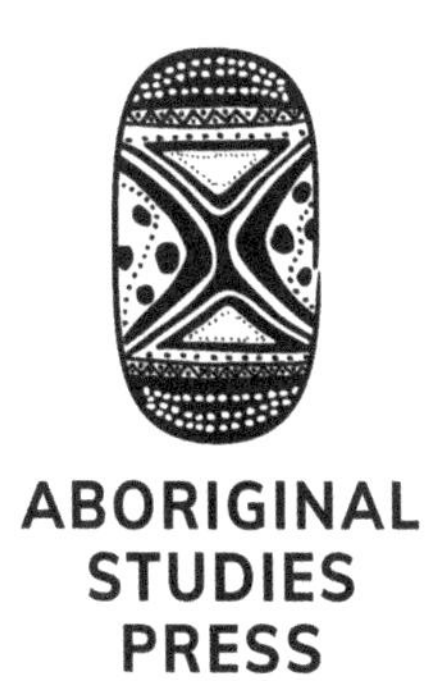

ABORIGINAL STUDIES PRESS

FIRST PUBLISHED IN 1999 BY
Aboriginal Studies Press
for the Australian Institute of Aboriginal and Torres Strait Islander Studies,
GPO Box 553, Canberra ACT 2601

NATIONAL LIBRARY OF AUSTRALIA CATALOGUING-IN-PUBLICATION DATA:

Eickelkamp, Ute.
"Don't ask for stories –": the women from Ernabella and their art.

ISBN 0 85575 310 2.

1. Aborigines, Australian – South Australia – Ernabella – Art. 2. Women artists – Australia – History. I. Title.

704.039915

EDITED BY Stephanie Haygarth, Canberra
DESIGNED BY Christine Bruderlin, Newcastle
PRODUCED BY Aboriginal Studies Press
COVER: photocollage by Nyuwara Tapaya

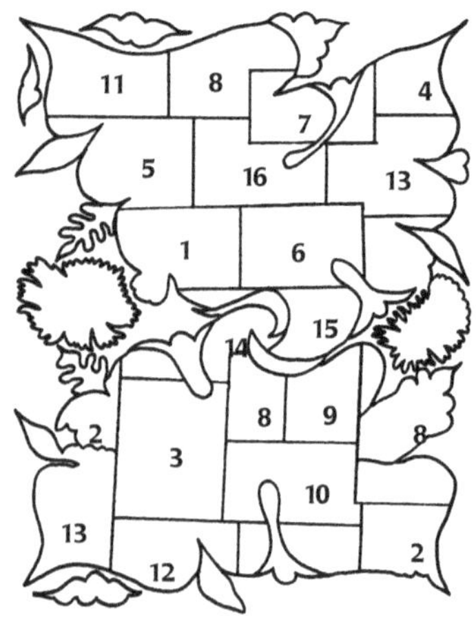

Key to front cover illustration

1. Hooked floor rug by Nyukana Baker, 1990s (Ernabella Arts collection)
2. Gouache on canvas, by Alison Carroll, 1990s (Michelle Swanborough collection, photograph Ute Eickelkamp)
3. Painting, acrylic on canvas by Unurupa Kulyuru, late 1980s or early 1990s (Ernabella Arts collection)
4. Silk painting (detail), by Alison Carroll, 1995 (Ernabella Arts collection, photograph Ute Eickelkamp)
5. Recent acrylic painting on paper, by Tjunkaya Tapaya (Ernabella Arts collection, photograph Ute Eickelkamp)
6. Acrylic painting on board, by Makinti Minutjukur, late 1960s or early 1970s (Ernabella church collection, photograph Ute Eickelkamp)
7. Acrylic painting on board, by Makinti Minutjukur, late 1960s or early 1970s (Presbyterian Church Trust Corporation collection, Victoria, photograph Ute Eickelkamp)
8. Silk batik, by Margaret Dagg, 1994 (photograph Ernabella Arts)
9. Batik by Atipalku Intjalki, 1993 (National Museum of Australia collection)
10. Batik by Nyukana Baker, 1989
11. Batik by Nungalka Stanley, 1989 (Ernabella Arts collection)
12. Batik, artist unknown
13. *Birds, feathers and nests/Tjulpuku nyalpu munu manngu*, by Nyuwara Tapaya, offset lithographic print on paper (Ernabella Arts collection)
14. *Old man waiting for the rain to stop/Tjilpi ngurangka nyinanyi kapiku patara*, by Elsie Taylor, offset lithographic print on paper (Ernabella Arts collection)
15. *Night-time*, by Elsie Taylor, offset lithographic print on paper (Ernabella Arts collection)
16. *My best design/Ngayuku walka wirunya*, by Angkuna Kulyuru, 1990s, lithographic offset print on paper (Ernabella Arts collection)

(Most works created in 1989 and 1996 with the exception of 6 and 7, which were probably done in the early 1970s.)

contents

Yangkuyi Yakiti

Tjulkiwa Atira Atira

Margaret Dagg

LEXIE

Nyukana Baker

NYUWARA TAPAYA

Nura RUPERT

NYINGUTA

Mayawara Minutjukur

Nungalka

Tjikalyi Colin.

Carol Williams

Atipalku Intjalki

DORA HAGGIE

AMANDA KOLYURU

Alec Minutjukur

Kanytjupai ARMSTRONG

L.W. Lester.

Makinti Minutjukur

how this project came into being

The Ernabella painting school was first brought to my attention in 1993 by Dr Ross Bowden, then an anthropologist at La Trobe University, Melbourne, who had donated his mother's collection of early Ernabella paintings to the National Gallery of Victoria. Two years later, in April 1995, I left Berlin to undertake anthropological field research about the Pitjantjatjara and Yankunytjatjara women's art school centred around the craftroom at Ernabella, a community of 500 people located at the southeastern end of the Musgrave Ranges in the north of South Australia.

The publication of this book is timely as the art centre at Ernabella celebrated its 50th anniversary in 1998. With its beginning in the drawing class of the first mission school, which had opened in 1940, and the foundation of the craftroom in 1949 (incorporated in 1974), the Ernabella women's art school is one of the longest established centres of contemporary Aboriginal art in Australia. It is best known for its outstanding and pioneering achievements in the batik medium, a technique that artists from Ernabella have taught in other Aboriginal communities in isolated areas.

Textile art appears to be developing into a regional genre of visual arts in Central Australia, which reflects the common artistic experiences of Aboriginal and non-Aboriginal women, while at the same time allowing for the expression of cultural and individual idiosyncrasies of style. Works from Ernabella, both historical and contemporary, feature in the collections of Australia's major public galleries and museums, as well as in private collections in this country and overseas. Western European ideas about what Aboriginal art is or should look like have not always allowed for the recognition of the distinct 'abstract' patterns created by Ernabella women, and have in the past led to a categorisation of the works, especially in textile media, as craft. Irrespective of external expectations, the artists have consistently explored their design style, which has grown into a tradition in its own right.

The idea of compiling a history of the artists was suggested to me by the coordinator of the Ngaatjatjarra Pitjantjatjara Yankunytjatjara Women's Council, Maggie Kavanagh, as a means of returning something valuable to the people with whom I worked during my doctoral studies. So, during the five months of my first stay in the community, I recorded over 20 life histories of women (and some men) who have been associated with Ernabella's art and craft production, with the intention of presenting them in book form.

However, such a literacy-based approach seemed not to match the basic aim of this history: to work with, and for the direct benefit of, the artists and their families. We therefore decided to adopt a primarily pictorial way of presenting the story of Ernabella arts, and the unique Ernabella design, supplemented by explanatory remarks. This idea was essentially inspired by numerous and lengthy conversations with Dr Gertrude Stotz, a Pitjantjatjara Council anthropologist, and Rob Burdon and Judy Torzillo, who have developed a computer graphics program based on icons that aims to solve cross-cultural communication problems.

I documented the narratives during my first spell of research, then we carried out this second stage of the project – putting it all together – between April and November 1996, when I returned to Ernabella. That's when the 'puzzle' really began. Having heard many stories about life on the former mission station (1937 to 1972); about times of transition when Ernabella became an independent community then named after its main Dreaming, Pukatja; about the decentralisation initiative (the so-called 'homeland movement'); and present-day problems, all of which form the background to an understanding of the women's artistic activity, I 'grazed' the many pages of transcribed interviews for seminal quotes. These I arranged in such a way as to gradually reconstruct the historical context of Ernabella arts from the artists' perspective. The results were then counterchecked with the participants of the project.

Not only did I keep the length and number of individual stories to an extent suitable for our purposes, but I also felt that the blending of quotes from several interviews would mirror the common practice of collaboratively telling a story. I also suggested reproducing a number of complete life histories in order to provide some coherent narratives of individual artists' experiences.

The first language of most speakers is Pitjantjatjara (or, of some, the related dialect Yankunytjatjara), but some conversations were held in English to adjust to my slowly increasing grasp of the vernacular. Translations into either Pitjantjatjara or English, depending on which was the original version of the text, were done by several women along the way, though Kanytjupai Armstrong, who is a trained bible interpreter, corrected and translated the bulk of the material. In the presentation of the text, the language of the original recording precedes its translation.

The Pitjantjatjara text conforms with the standard spelling system, as in Cliff Goddard's *Pitjantjatjara/Yankunytjatjara to English Dictionary* (Institute for Aboriginal Development, 1992), with the only difference being that retroflex sounds are not underlined. This omission is common in printed material designed for Anangu readers.

The artists advised me not to translate the table of contents, my introduction and the acknowledgements, and the glossary, as they form my contribution to the book and therefore belong to my language, or rather, German being my mother tongue, to a sphere clearly separate from theirs.

Types of speech vary greatly across the book and have not been 'whitewashed', so that the character and purpose of the diverse levels and contexts of communication have been maintained. Kanytjupai Armstrong nevertheless adjusted the oral narratives to the requirements of a written text so as to ensure coherence and comprehensibility. The reviewed stories were then counterchecked with the narrators, who provided additional information – sometimes generated during discussions with other listeners present at these occasions – or who requested parts to be deleted for publication purposes.

Together we selected photographs and other illustrative material to accompany the quotes, or vice versa, a process resembling the composition of the designs at which these artists excel. The idea of presenting the craftroom story in the form of a 'dot-painting' – a technique and iconography adopted by Ernabella artists during the 1980s from other Western Desert and Central Australian groups – so as to include illiterate people into the group of 'readers', was suggested by Marie Warren, the studio's screenprinter. Makinti Minutjukur took on the task and created her own stunning version in a painting.

The story of the developmental stages of the craftroom, including relevant dates and introductions to art techniques and materials, is based on published material by and personal communication with Winifred Hilliard, who supervised the craftroom for 32 years, and personal communication with Mary Bennett, Ernabella's first official craft coordinator.

Reverend Ron Trudinger, the first schoolteacher (*c* 1940–45) and later superintendent of the mission (1949–57), and Reverend Bill Edwards, superintendent from 1958 to 1972 and secretary and interpreter for the Pitjantjatjara Council during land rights negotiations from 1976 to 1980, were both generous in sharing their professional and personal experiences in the course of our conversations. Reverend Edwards also proofread the manuscript. Information on the recent history of Ernabella Arts was provided by Jenni Dudley, the art coordinator there while I was doing my fieldwork, whose continuous practical and intellectual support has been indispensable for the project. Vivid descriptions by Anangu of everyday life on the mission and of the evolvement of their arts were assembled along this skeletal storyline to make it become alive again.

The first part of the title of this book, *'Don't Ask for Stories . . .'*, is a quote from an interview held in English with Tjikalyi Tjapiya who, like the other artists, repeatedly explained to me that their design is not a narrative or a topical one. But there are many stories behind the development of the Ernabella women's art school, and this is the *raison d'être* of this book: to share their lives and works with a wider audience. The second part of the title, *The Women from Ernabella and Their Art*, originally in Pitjantjatjara, was created by Tjikalyi Tjapiya, Angkuna Kulyuru and myself, during a discussion about whom we wanted the book to address and what the main message should be. The translation was collaboratively produced with assistance from Kanytjupai Armstrong.

As I've already mentioned, the combination of visual and literal accounts was chosen in order to communicate the story of Ernabella arts to Aboriginal and non-Aboriginal people alike. However, I did not intend to diminish the status of the art by using it as an educational tool, a risk pointed out to me by art critics, who have engaged in the complex discourse of objectively categorising and redefining Aboriginal art.

This is a story from the 'inside', an attempt at documenting the coming into being of the Ernabella art school as seen by those who have been part of it – a joint project. Not all the women whose lives and work are written into the history of the craftroom could be represented in this book, but it is to the credit of each single one of them that they have kept this artistic tradition going and growing, taking it with them as they travelled on. Thank you all for teaching me!

I would also like to thank other 'invisibles' here, because without them, the project would not have come into being. They are the Australian Institute of Aboriginal and Torres Strait Islander Studies for having funded the research, and Mary Edmunds and Stephen Wild in particular for their open-mindedness and flexibility in responding to our needs; Anangu Pitjantjatjara (AP), and the Pitjantjatjara Council for granting access to their technical infrastructure and services 'out bush' and in Alice Springs (the latter also provided a substantial sum for transcripts done by the Institute for Aboriginal Development), and the Pitjantjatjara Council's Aṟa Irititja Archival Project for providing photographic material. I am also deeply indebted to Gertrude Stotz, for her academic and practical advice in the field and beyond; Elizabeth Köpping and Peter Köpping for their patient supervision in and from Germany; and my family and friends both in Germany and Australia, for their financial assistance, advice and constant encouragement.

Ute Eickelkamp
Research and coordination

list of contributors

(in alphabetical order)

Nyukana Baker
Kunmanara Brumby
Tjikalyi Tjapiya
Alison Curley
Margaret Dagg
Wally Dunn
Dora Haggie
Lexie Ingkatji
Tjulkiwa Kunmanara
Lucy Lester
Alec Minutjukur
Makinti Minutjukur
Mayawara Minutjukur
Kutungu (Betty) Kunmanara
Marissa Kunmanara
Peter Nyaningu
Angkaliya Purampi
Nura Rupert
Nungalka Stanley
Nura Ward
Marie Warren
Yangkuyi Yakiti

compiler's note

In the presentation of the text of *'Don't Ask for Stories . . .'*, the language of the original recording precedes its translation, appearing in the left column. Translations into either Pitjantjatjara or English, depending on which was the original version of the text, were done by several women along the way, though Kanytjupai Armstrong, who is a trained bible interpreter, corrected and translated the bulk of the material.

maps

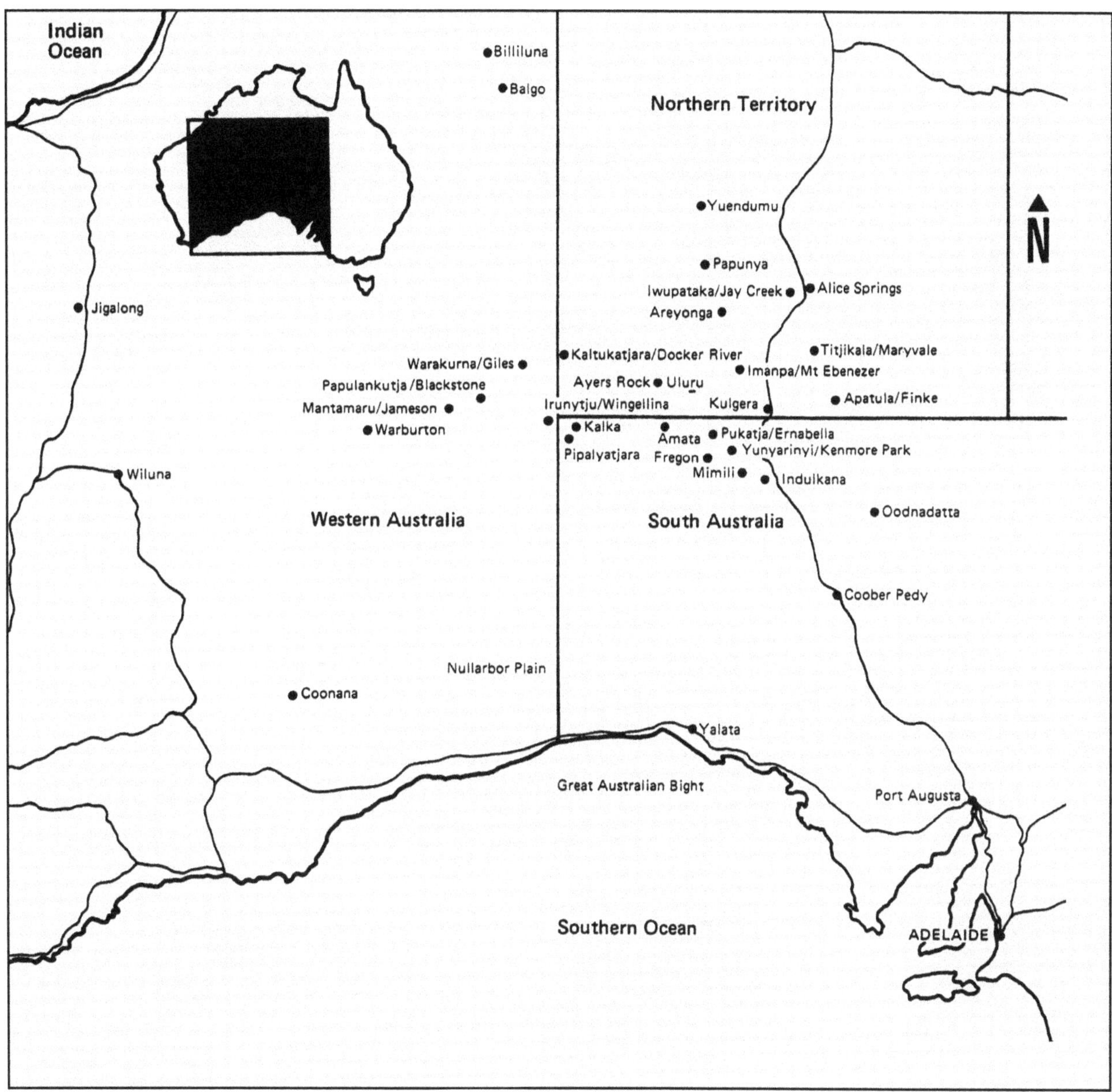

Map 1. Locations of speakers of Western Desert dialects (reproduced with permission from P Eckert and J Hudson, *Wangka Wiru: A Handbook for the Pitjantjatjara Language Learner,* University of South Australia, 1994)

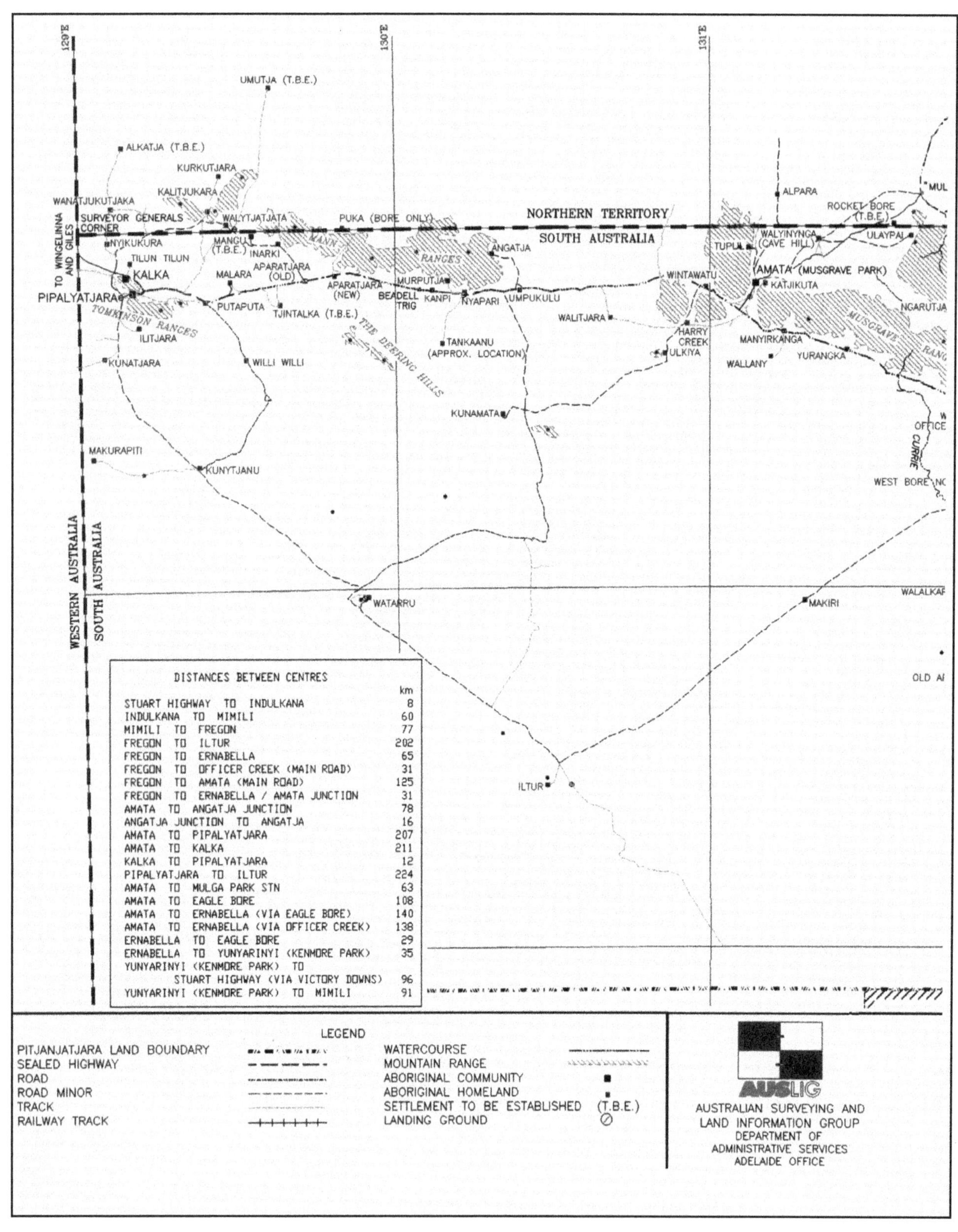

Map 2. Communities and homelands on Anangu Pitjantjatjara lands (© Commonwealth of Australia, AUSLIG, Australia's national mapping agency. All rights reserved.)

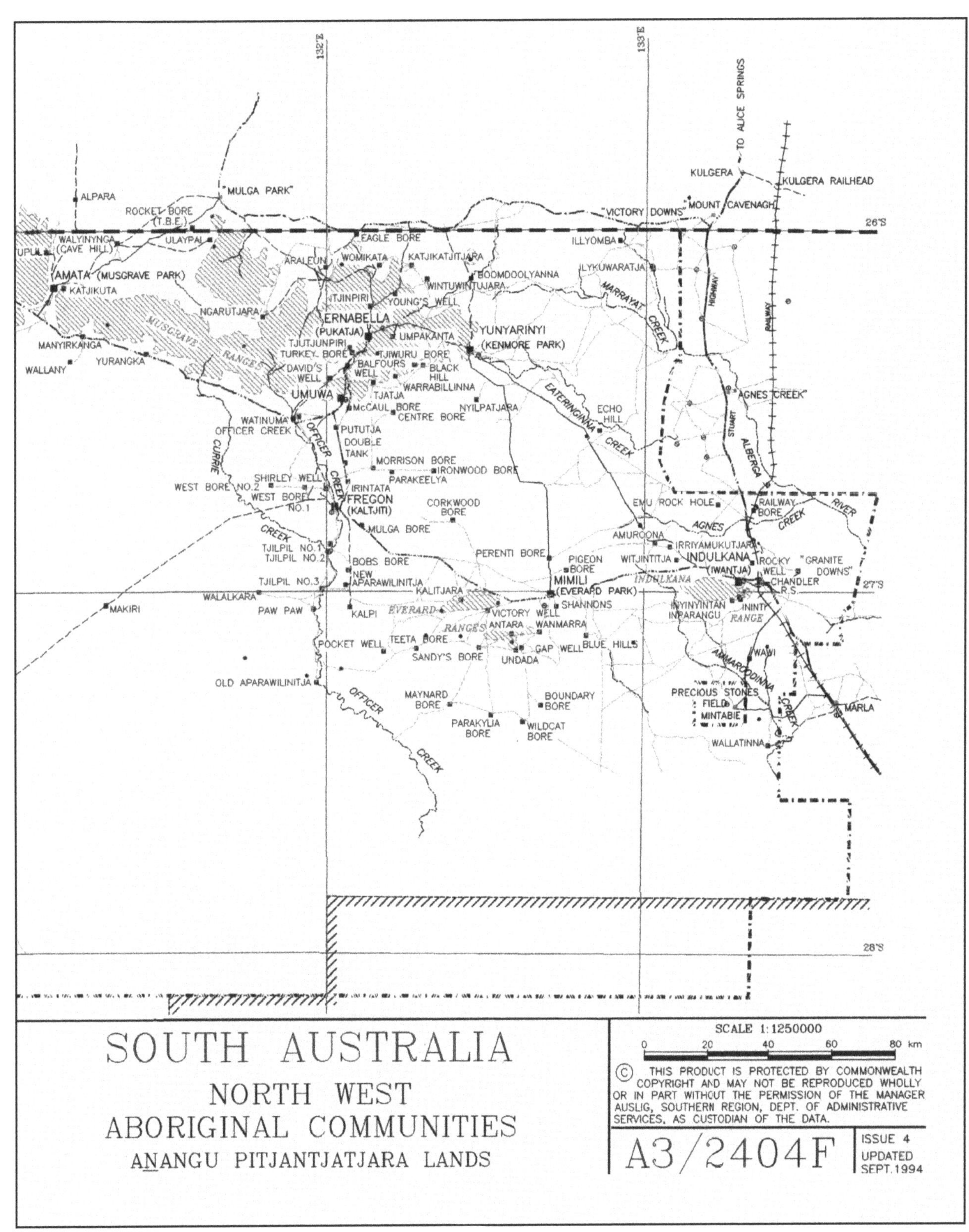
132°E
133°E
26°S
27°S
28°S
TO ALICE SPRINGS
KULGERA
KULGERA RAILHEAD
"VICTORY DOWNS"
MOUNT CAVENAGH
ALPARA
"MULGA PARK"
ROCKET BORE (T.B.E.)
WALYINYNGA (CAVE HILL)
ULAYPAI
EAGLE BORE
ILLYOMBA
AMATA (MUSGRAVE PARK)
KATJIKUTA
ARALEUN
WOMIKATA
KATJIKATJITJARA
BOOMDOOLYANNA
LYKUWARATJA
WINTUWINTUJARA
MARRAYAT CREEK
HIGHWAY
RAILWAY
NGARUTJARA
ITJINPIRI
YOUNG'S WELL
MUSGRAVE RANGES
ERNABELLA (PUKATJA)
UMPAKANTA
YUNYARINYI (KENMORE PARK)
TJUTJUNPIRI
TURKEY BORE
TJIWURU BORE
MANYIRKANGA
WALLANY
YURANGKA
DAVID'S WELL
BALFOURS WELL
BLACK HILL
WARRABILLINNA
UMUWA
TJATJA
McCAUL BORE
CENTRE BORE
NYILPATJARA
EATERINGINNA CREEK
ECHO HILL
"AGNES CREEK"
STUART
ALBERGA
WATINUMA
OFFICER CREEK
PUTUTJA
DOUBLE TANK
CURRIE
MORRISON BORE
IRONWOOD BORE
PARAKEELYA
SHIRLEY WELL
WEST BORE NO.2
WEST BORE NO.1
IRINTATA
FREGON (KALTJITI)
CORKWOOD BORE
EMU ROCK HOLE
RAILWAY BORE
RIVER
AGNES CREEK
MULGA BORE
AMUROONA
IRRIYAMUKUTJARA
TJILPIL NO.1
TJILPIL NO.2
BOBS BORE
PERENTI BORE
PIGEON BORE
WITJINTITJA
INDULKANA (IWANTJA)
ROCKY WELL
"GRANITE DOWNS"
TJILPIL NO.3
NEW APARAWILINITJA
MIMILI (EVERARD PARK)
INDULKANA
CHANDLER R.S.
WALALKARA
KALITJARA
MAKIRI
PAW PAW
KALPI
EVERARD RANGES
VICTORY WELL
SHANNONS
INYINYINTAN
INPARANGU
ININTI
RANGE
ANTARA
WANMARRA
POCKET WELL
TEETA BORE
GAP WELL
BLUE HILLS
WAWI
SANDY'S BORE
UNDADA
AMAROODINNA CREEK
OLD APARAWILINITJA
OFFICER CREEK
MAYNARD BORE
BOUNDARY BORE
PRECIOUS STONES FIELD
MINTABIE
MARLA
PARAKYLIA BORE
WILDCAT BORE
WALLATINNA
SOUTH AUSTRALIA
NORTH WEST
ABORIGINAL COMMUNITIES
ANANGU PITJANTJATJARA LANDS
SCALE 1:1250000
0 20 40 60 80 km
© THIS PRODUCT IS PROTECTED BY COMMONWEALTH COPYRIGHT AND MAY NOT BE REPRODUCED WHOLLY OR IN PART WITHOUT THE PERMISSION OF THE MANAGER AUSLIG, SOUTHERN REGION, DEPT. OF ADMINISTRATIVE SERVICES, AS CUSTODIAN OF THE DATA.
A3/2404F
ISSUE 4
UPDATED SEPT.1994

1

living in the bush
putingka nyinanytja

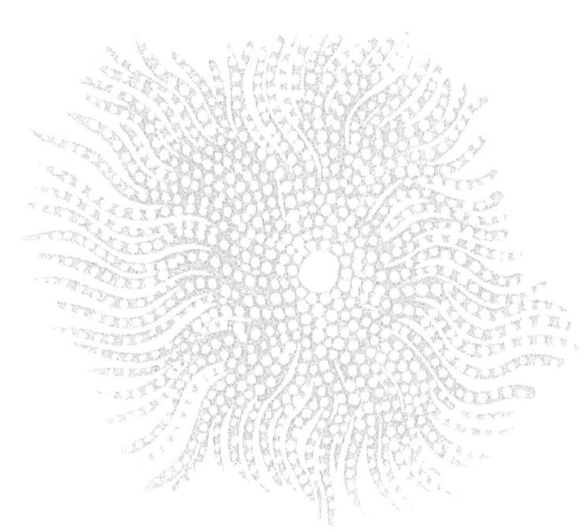

SOMEONE CARING FOR US
KUTJUPANGKU NGANANANYA KANYININGI

Alec Minutjukur
(Translation by Kanytjupai Armstrong)

I think, in my days, someone caring for us, looking after us, someone was there all the time. God was looking after us when we were living in the bush.

When we come to know the white people, old people were living there all their life, no sicknesses, a lot of walking, long way. It might be hundred mile walking, two hundred mile. The grandmothers were given the children to look after when parents go hunting.

Ngayulu kulini malakukutura ngayulu panya nyinanytja kutjupangkulanya wirura kanyiningi atunymara rawangka nyangatja tjukurpa mulapa panya Godalu ngananya atunymara kanyiningi ngananana putingka watarku nyinanyangka.

Palula nguru ngananana piranpa tjutaku nintiringu kaya pampa munu tjilpi tjuta pika wiya. Pukulpa alatjitu nyinangi munuya ngura parari ankupai tjina mutuka wiyangka kalanya kami tjutangku tjitji tjuta kanyilpai mama ngunytju kukaku ankunyangka.

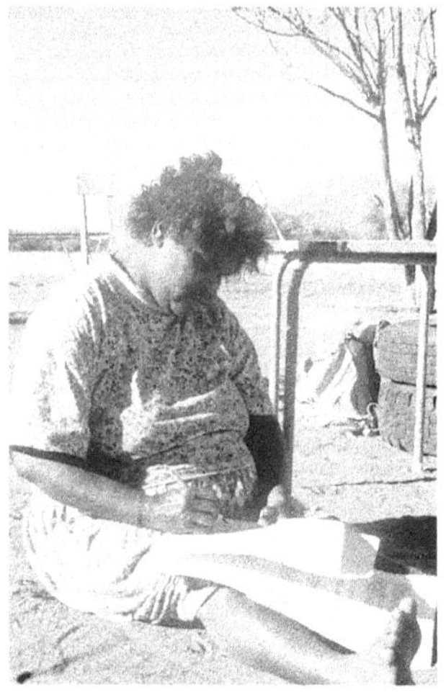

Kanytjupai Armstrong translating for the book, 1996 (photograph Ute Eickelkamp)

LIVING IN A BUSH HUT
WILTJANGKA NYINANYI

Nura Rupert

(Translation by Ute Eickelkamp)

Minyma nyangatja ananyi piti tjalira mina tjukulangka tjitji tjutangku tjikintjaku, unganyi tjikintjaku. Munu wiltjangka unytjunta unganyi ka tjana tjikini tjitji tjutangku tjikira wiyaringkula malu ngalkuni, munuya pukulpa nyinanyi.

Ka wati ananyi kuka maluku,

The woman goes to fetch water for the children to drink, carrying a wooden dish on her head in which to transport the water. And back in the hut, she gives the water to her children and they drink it, and when they have stilled their thirst, they eat kangaroo meat, and they are happy.

Large traditional bush hut/ Wiltja pulka irititja, by Nura Rupert (Ute Eickelkamp collection)

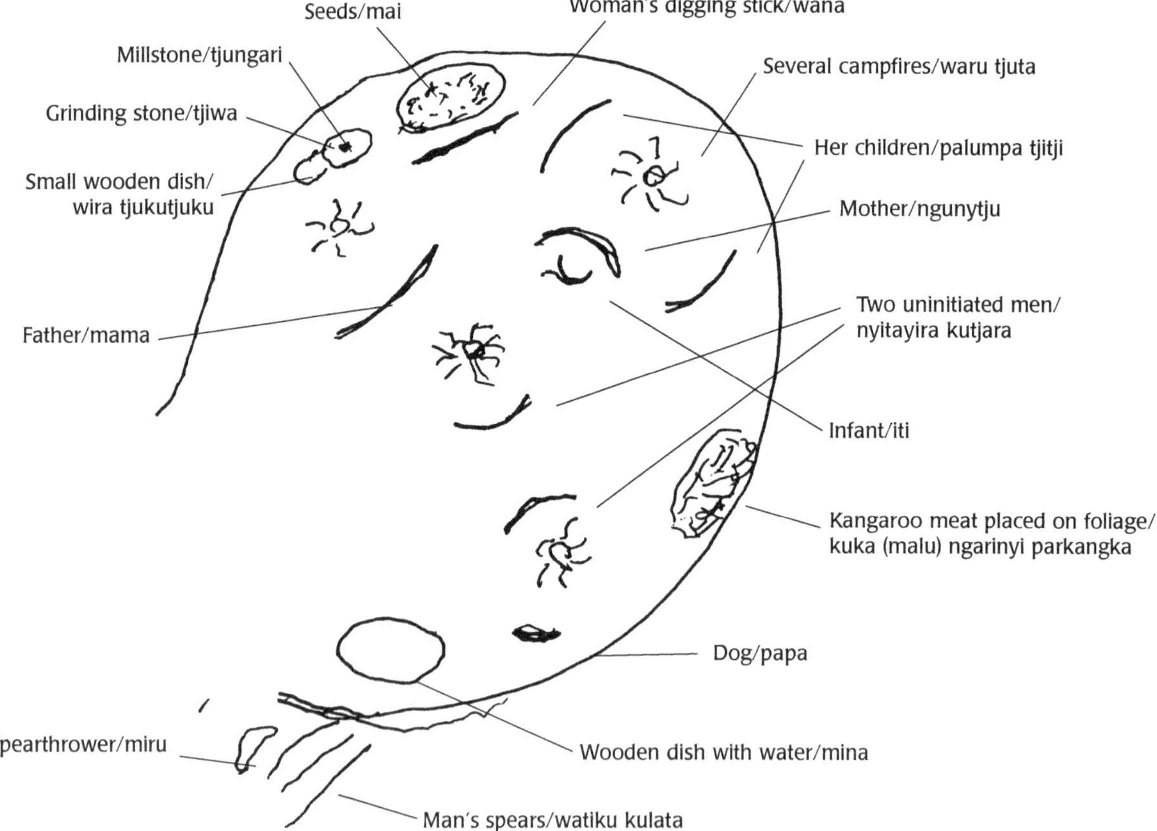

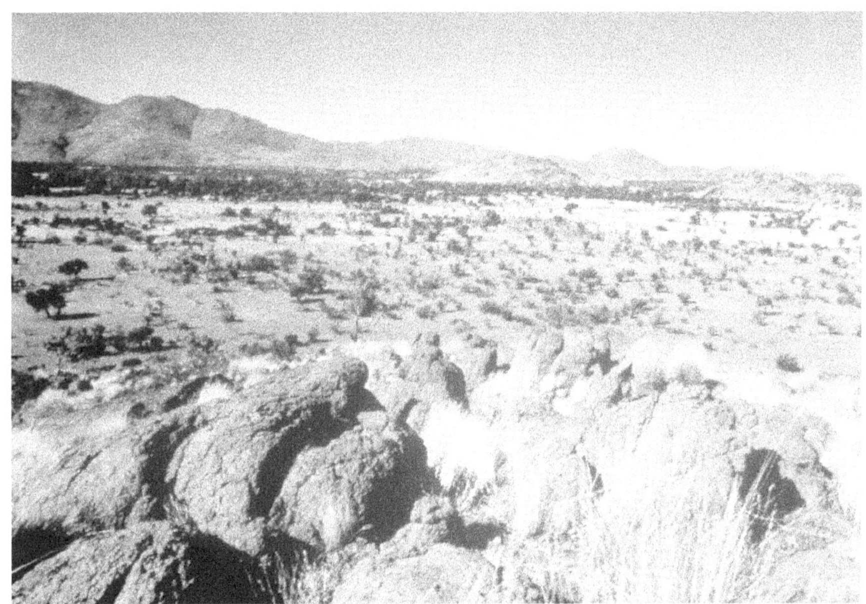

Looking southeast from Ernabella, through the Musgrave Ranges (photograph Ute Eickelkamp)

Remains of a traditional shelter around 30 years old, 1995 (photograph Ute Eickelkamp)

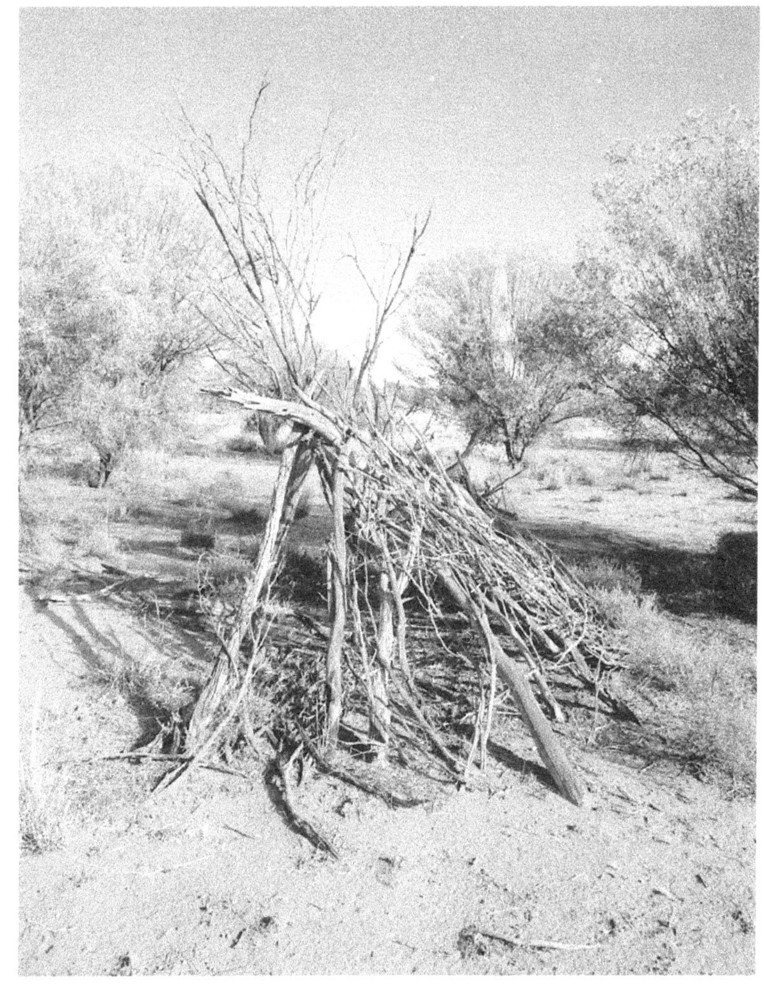

kulata mantjini, miru mantjini munu ananyi kukaku. Mungartji pitjanyi kuka nyuti katinyi. Munu tjitji tjutangku wangkanyi, 'Mamalu, malu katinyi!', munu pukulpa tjana.

Munu wati waru palyani munu pauni kuka panya ka tjankaringkunyangka mantjini munu parkangka tjunanyi munu tjunta kutjara palyani mirungka. Munu witapi angkalpa tjunanyi parkangka tjitji tjuta ngalkuntjaku. Munu watingku miru mantjira kuka palyanu ka tjitjingku tjikini malu milkali munu kunpuringanyi.

Tjukurpa irititja nyangatja.

Minyma ankupai piti tjalira tjukulangka mina tjutintjikitja tjitjingku tjikintjaku, munu katangku tjalira katipai ngurakutu. Munu wiltjangka unytjunta ungkupai mina tjikintjaku kaya tjikira wiyaringkula malangka malu ngalkupai munuya pukulpa nyinapai.

Ka wati ankupai kuka maluku, kulata miru mantjira munu mungartji pitjapai kuka nyutitjara kaya tjitji tjutangku wangkapai, 'Mamalu, malu nganampa katinyi!', munu pukularipai. Ka watingku panya waru tilira malu panya paulpai munu tjankaringkunyangka mantjira tjirpikangka tjunkula palyalpai mirungka.

Munu witapi angkalpa tjunkupai tjirpikangka tjitji tjutangku ngalkuntjaku. Munu watingku miru mantjira kuka palyalpai mirungka ka tjitjingku milkali tjikilpai kunpu nyinanytjikitjangku.

Tjukurpa irititja nyangatja.

And the man goes hunting for kangaroo, taking his spears and spearthrower [a multi-purpose tool]. He returns from his hunt in the late afternoon, carrying the speared kangaroo bundled up on his head. And the children call out, 'Great, our father is bringing meat for us!', and they are happy.

And the man makes a fire and cooks that kangaroo and, when it is ready, he takes it out and places it on some branches, and he lays the two thighs in his spearthrower. And the back section of the kangaroo and the two hip sections he puts on another 'plate' of branches for the children to eat. And the man cuts into the meat with his miru to release the blood which the children drink, and they become strong.

This is a story about the past.

(The second, refined Pitjantjatjara version of Nura Rupert's story is by Margaret Dagg, who pointed out that the extreme simplicity of both language and storyline of the first mirror neither the narrator's general mode of speech, which is that of a senior woman, nor the complexity of the issue, that is, an account of a lifestyle. Instead, Nura adjusted the story to meet Ute Eickelkamp's very limited grasp of Pitjantjatjara. Margaret improved the language level so as to avoid a severe misrepresentation of the storyteller's narrative skills, but did not elaborate on the contents because it reflects the way knowledge is linguistically adjusted when passing it on to children.)

2

white man is coming (nura rupert's story)
wati piranpa pitjantja (nura rupertaku tjukurpa)

Nura Rupert
(recorded by Ute Eickelkamp, transcribed by the Institute for Aboriginal Development, corrected by Kanytjupai Armstrong, translated by Kanytjupai Armstrong and Ute Eickelkamp, proofread by Nura Rupert, Nyuwara Tapaya, Atipalku Intjalki and Edna Rupert)

Tjana anu Anapala missiontanguru ka wati piranpa anu kamulangka munu mai pulka mulapa katingi pulangkita kulu kulu anangu tjutaku munu ankula paluru wirkanu ananguku ngurangka munu waru kutjaningi anangu maru tjutangku nyakunytjaku palu tjana kumpira nyinangi tjanampa panya miri maru. Ka wati paluru waru kutjaningi tjana waru nyakula pitjantjaku palu tjana maru tjuta nguluringangi piranpa nyakula. Munu paluru tjana kumpira nyinangi munuya ngulungku nyangangi, kulira 'Nyaa nyaratja nyinanyi?'.

Kaya tjara ngulu wirtjapakanu panya tjana kamula nyangu palu paluru tjana anangu palunya tjananya mantjintjikitja pitjangu. Munu ngulytjuntjikitja Mr MacDougalltu panya wati maru kutjara kulu katingi alpamilantjaku munu mukuringangi anangu nyara

They left Ernabella mission by camel and rode out into the country, taking a lot of food, blankets and other things with them. When they arrived, they lit a fire and the black people hid behind bushes. They made fire and smoke to attract Aboriginal people who were observing the white people, watching from their hiding places, being scared and thinking, 'What is this, who is making that fire?'.

And they ran away when they saw the camels. The white people had come to catch Aboriginal people, they were searching for black people. Mr MacDougall and two Aboriginal men helped to 'catch' Anangu: they wanted those people to come, so they made a fire in the creekbed. He made camp near a soakage that was the only waterhole in Ernabella. That's where he stayed.

People came to drink there and then they returned to their bushcamps

tjanampa munu waru kutjaningi karungka panya paluru mina piti nyakula waru kutjanu ka mina piti kutju Anapalala ngarangi.

Ka anangu tjutangku ngura nyara palulanguru mina tjikiningi munu paluru tjana ankula nyinapai yuu wirungka wiltja wirungka. Munu paluru tjana mungawinkiringkula kukaku ankupai, emuku munuya malu tjuta wakalpai. Kaya minyma tjutangku mai wiru tjuta mantjilpai, kunakanti, wakati, kaltu kaltu, mai putitja wiru tjuta paluru tjana mantjilpai. Munu paluru tjana katira kanira unytjunytju wiyara kilinara tjiwangka tjunkula rungkara tjitji tjuta ungkupai. Paluru tjana rawangku rungkara rungkara wirangka tjunkula warungka tjunkupai mai kaya tjitji tjutaku ngunytjungka para nyinara wanara ngalkupai. Mai palulanguru dampa pulka palyalpai munu paulpai tjanampa tjitji panya tjutaku munu katara tjananya ungkupai. Kaya ngalkula paltjaringkupai panya tjana mai wirungka pulkaringu bushtuckangka [mai putitjangka].

Mai wiru ngalkulaya pukulpa nyinapai ka mama tjuta ankupai munu malu emu kulu kulu wakara katipai munu tjitji tjuta paltjalpai. Kaya yuu wirungka paluru tjana nyinapai waru pulkangka ngura unytjunta pulangkita wiyangka palu tjana panya waru kampa kutjara tjunkupai tjana waru ngururpa kulu kutjalpai kalala kulku palyantjikitjangku munu mungaringkula kulku palunya lipilpai unytjunpa ngarinytjikitjangku.

Ka wiltja wiru ngarapai. Tenta wiya blanket wiya uwankara wiru kunpu paluru tjana nyinapai pika wiya kutjupa kutjupa tjuta wiyangka, pika wiya, alatjitu. Kutjupa kutjupa tjuta mantjintja wiya paluru tjana

and went hunting for emu and kangaroo, and the women collected grass seeds – kunakanti, wakati, kaltu kaltu – bushfood which they brought back to the camp, where they ground it into powder on a stone to make damper out of it, baked in hot ashes. The mother and children sat in a semicircle and together they had their meal. They used to make a large damper from these seeds for all the children, and it was cut into pieces and shared. Everybody was satisfied and the children grew well on this bushfood. It is a nutritious diet and everyone was in good health.

The fathers went hunting kangaroos with their spears, and the children were always being fed. And they sat behind a windbreak at a big fire to keep everyone warm, as there were no blankets. A fire was made at each side of two windbreaks set up opposite each other, and a third big fire in the centre. At night-time, the ashes of the large fire were pushed aside and people slept on the warm sand that was loosened up to form a shallow depression filled with soft warm sand.*

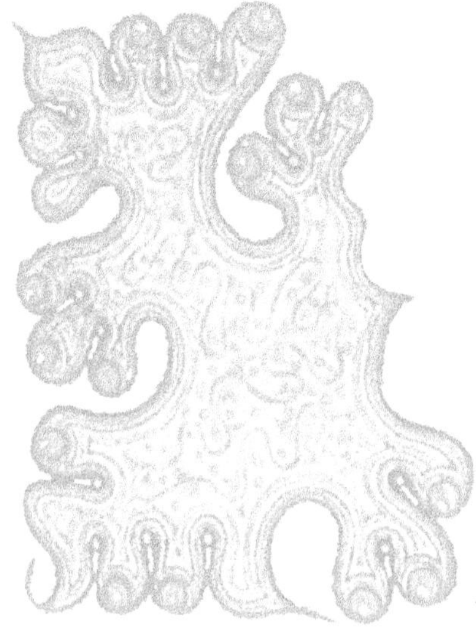

** Information by Kanytjupai Armstrong and Margaret Dagg; still practised occasionally as seen by Ute Eickelkamp.*

akuri akuri nyinapai pukulpa warka pulka palyara ka tjitji paluru tjana pulkaringkula watiringkula munu kungkawararingu palya alatjitu uwankara.* Munu kutjupa kutjupa pika kanyintja wiya mai nyanga putitjanguru mai wiru kutju wangununguru kaltu kaltunguru kunakantinguru wakatinguru ilinguru.

Do you think the new food like flour, tea and sugar brought many diseases and problems?

Nyanga paluru tjana pika kanyini palu mai nyanga nganampa nguru miritjina wiru, bush medicine, bush tucka mai nyara paluru tjana mai palya mulapa mangata tjuta wakati tjuta kulu. Tjana pukulpa nyinapai pika wiya kutjupa kutjupa mantjintja wiya unngu pika kanyintja wiya pukulpa alatjitu.

Ka tjana kamula tjuta pitjangu wati panya Dr Duguidatjara munu Mr MacDougallnga munupula wati maru kutjara kulu ngalyakatingu munu paluru tjana waru tiliningi anangu tjuta ngulytjuntjikitjangku munuya tinta pitatjura mai kuntara kuka puluka kulu kulu mai tjamangkara palunya tjananya ungangi. Kaya paluru tjana pitjangu munuya ngulu ngulu tjitji wati minyma kulu kulu uwankara patu nyinangi. Ka tjananya wati paluru altingu 'Pitjaya! Nyurampa mai nyangatja'. Panya Dr Duguidalu munu Mr MacDougallalu pula tjananya ngulytjuningi puyungka anangu panya tjuta altira.

Panya Dr Duguidanya wangka Pitjantjatjaraku ninti wiya iriti panya paluru Ingkilitja kutju wangkapai Pitjantjatjara ngurpa. Ka Mr MacDougallanya kutju

Their life was without illness and pain and people were healthy and worked and were happy. They grew into strong young men and women without any diseases because of their good diet, consisting of wangunu, kaltu kaltu, kunakanti, wakati and figs.

Do you think the new food like flour, tea and sugar brought many diseases and problems?

We became sick from the new food whereas our food is good medicine, bush medicine. Bushfood is nutritious, like mangata and wakati, and people were living well without internal diseases.

Then they brought the camel, that was Dr Duguid and Mr MacDougall and two Anangu men. They lit a fire to attract Anangu so they could catch them and they set up camp, a tent, blankets and jam, and they spread out the bread and meat and gave it to Anangu. Children, men and women carefully came closer, but they were in fear. And Dr Duguid and Mr MacDougall called out to them, 'Come

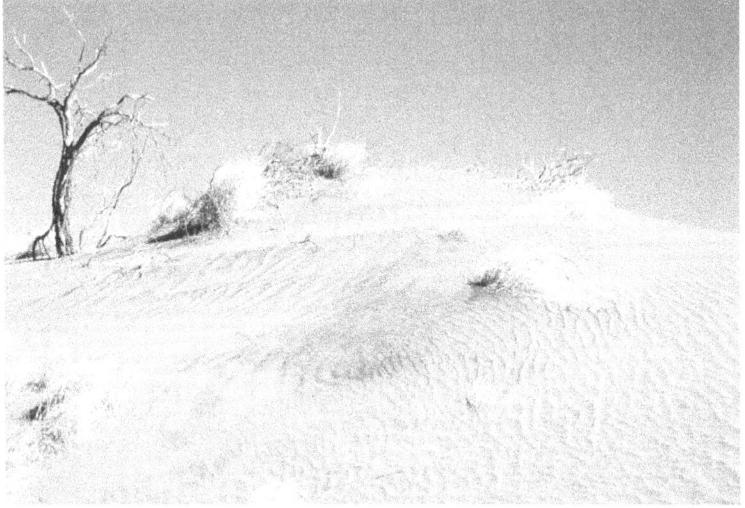

Womikata, sand dune near Ernabella, children's playground, 1995 (photograph Ute Eickelkamp)

Pitjantjatjaraku tjukutjuku ninti munu wangkangu anangu tjutangka alatji: 'Pitjamaya, nyurampa mai nyangatja!'. Kaya pitjala ila nyinara wananu palu tjana tjitji wati minyma kulu kulu nyinangi kaya wati tjuta kulata tjunkula pitjala nyinakatingu mai ngalkunytjikitjangku. Panya tjana tjuta ngurangka wantikatingu wira tjiwa kulu kulu wantikatingu uwankara ngurangka. Panya tjana mai ready rungkara paura tjitji tjuta paltjantjikitjangku tjiwa tjungari kulata miru kuka maluku kanyilpai. Munu tjana pitjala nyinara ngulu ngulungku nyangangi.
Ka Mr MacDougallalu munu Dr Duguidalu pula wangkangu mai nyangatja nyurampa ngalkunmaya mai nyurampa nyangatja. Ka tjana wantingi munuya nguluringangi ka tjanaya pulangkita tjuta ungangi tiritja tjuta tarawatja tjarta kulu kulu tjananya ungangi tjarpantjaku palu tjana arara malakungku mantangka tjunangi. Tjinguru tjana ngurpangku putu kuliningi. Nganampa kami tjamu tjutangku.

Ngayulu wiya, Walternya tjana mamanya ngunytjunya tjana nyinangi tjuta paluru tjana mama ngunytjungka nyinangi. Munu Nganyinytjanya ngayuku kuntiliku untalpa panya Angatjala nyinanyi paluru tjana nyinangi ngura Kanpila itingka ngura nyara paluru panya ngayuku mamaku nyara palulaya nyinangi nikiti paluru tjana pukulpa, wiltja wirutjara ka tjananya tarawatja tjarta ungangi palunya tjananya ka paluru tjana putu tjarpangi tarawatjangka ngurpa ngaltutjara kuwari kutju paluru ngulytjuningi, wati nyangangku palu Mr MacDougallalu kulu mai ungangi tarawatja pulangkita kulu. Ka

over here, there's food for you!'. They had made a fire and smoke to attract the people and then they all approached the camp.

Dr Duguid (they later taught him Pitjantjatjara) spoke only English and Mr MacDougall, who knew some Pitjantjatjara, said, 'Here is your food!'. And they all sat in one line; the men, having brought their hunting spears, laid them down beside them on the ground. They had left all other tools and gadgets, such as spearthrowers and grinding stones, safely at their camp ready to be used to provide food for the children. They were scared and they kept looking at the white people.
Mr MacDougall and Dr Duguid called out to them, ' Here is something to eat for you!'. And they were given blankets, dresses, trousers, shirts and other things. They picked them up and threw them back on the ground. Maybe our grandparents tried to understand what these things were but they had never seen them before and could not make sense of them.

I didn't see all this happen, but my brother, Walter, and my parents witnessed the scene. They used to live near Kanpi, around Angatja, in my father's country with Nganyinytjanya and her mother, my aunty. They lived without clothes, but they had good bush shelters and they were happy. They were naked and when they were offered trousers, the poor things didn't know how to put them on.
Mr MacDougall, who came out west, was the first white person they had ever seen. He gave them food and blankets, but they didn't know how to use white man's things, but they learnt to wear trousers.

paluru tjana putu kuliningi munuya ngulalta ma nintiringkula tjarpangi tarawatjangka.

Ka tjananya Anapalalakutu katingu kutjupatjara Ayers Rockalakutu katingu tjara kutjupa kamulangka. Ayers Rockalakutu katingu munu tjara kutjupa ngalya katingu ka tjana nintiringkula ngalya wanara wirkanu ngura nyanga Anapalalakutu ngura nyanga paluru mission ngarangi iriti, mission time.

Missiontu alpamilanu wati tjukurtjara tjutangku munu paluru tjana pitjala nyinangi ka Dr Duguidanya Mr MacDougallnya pula ngura nyanga palula nyinangi munu paluru tjana tjunu wali mankurpa. Wali kutju munu mai ration ungkupai munuya church wiltja palyanu munulanya churchangka nintiningi anangu tjuta.

Ka ngayunya iti kulunypa katingu Kanpilanguru ngunytjungku ngayunya katingi iti ka ngayuku kuta tjitji pulka nyinka pulka malu wakalpai paluru mamangka tjungungku tjana kulatangka kutju wakaningi raipula wiyangka iriti munu paluru tjana kuka nyuti katira wanipai kala pukultu ngalkulpai ngayulu iti kulunypa pitjangi Anapalalakutu ngayunya katingu ngayuku ngunytju mamangku ka ngayulu wirkanu nyangangka iti kulunypa Anapalala. Nganana tjitji pulkaringu ngura nyangangka munula mai wiya nyinangi ka ration tjukutjuku tjunu wati tjukurtjarangku panya mission ngarangi ngura nyanga palula iriti. Ka nganana rations mantjilpai mai tjukutjuku panya nganana mai mantjilpai tjitji pulkaringkula kutju.

Ngayulu pulkaringu munu ngayulu kuulangka tjarpangi nganana

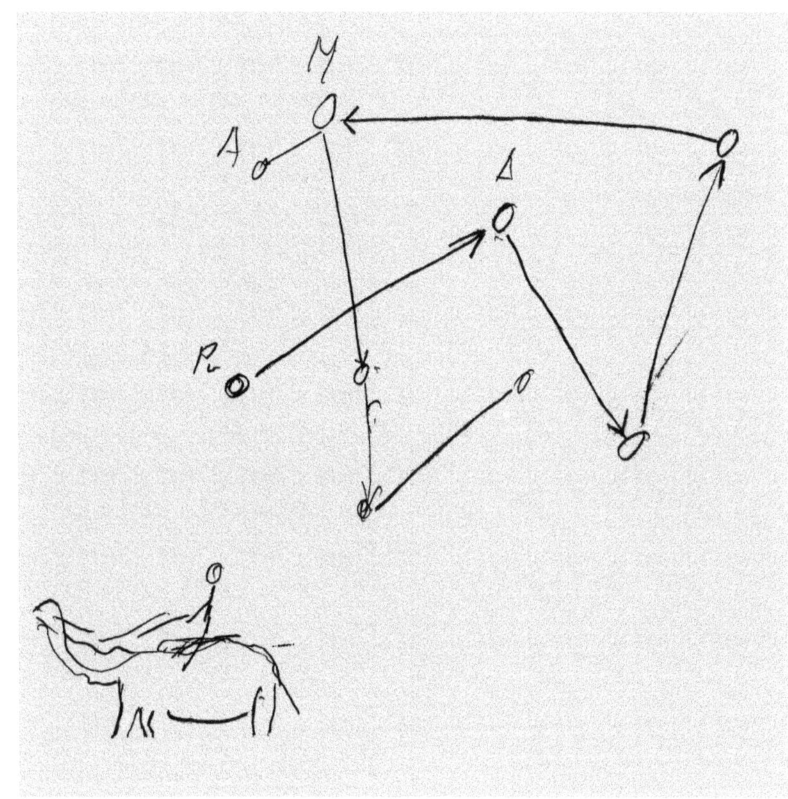

When the white man came on camel. . ., by Peter Nyaningu (showing traditional travel routes through places that are now communities), pencil on paper, 1996 (Ute Eickelkamp collection)

And they brought them to Ernabella while others went to Ayers Rock, following the man on the camel. People followed the white man, whom they had got to know, to Ernabella, the place that became a mission then.

Anangu helped setting up the mission – men and women became church leaders and ministers. The missionaries came and lived amongst Anangu. Dr Duguid and Mr MacDougall built three little houses, one of which was the ration shed. The church was a wiltja and Anangu learnt about the church.

I was a little baby when my mother brought me here from Kanpi. My older brother was a young man knowledgable of hunting. He used to go hunting with our father using spears, as they had no rifles in those days. They carried the game on their heads back to the camp and they

tjitji uwankara ka Dr Duguidanya nganampa teacher number one nyinangi nganmanypa.** Kuulangka nganana nyinangi munula tjitji pulkaringu nganana tjuta munu nganana milka cownguru mantjilpai goata tjutanguru kulu ka ngananya milkara ungkupai ngananyapanya minyma panya kutjungku warkaringkupaingku bucketangka para ungkupai. Kala nganana tjikilpai panya bridge ngaranyi panya apungka panya tjuwangka itingka nganana nyinapai tjitji tjuta waru kutjara ka ngananya nyara palula ungkupai. Munu nganana tjintu kutu mulapa ankupai kuulakutu ka nganampa waru kutjalpai munu towela ready tjunkupai comb kulu kulu. Munu ngananya kurpilpai hoseangka ka nganana paltjira paltjira tjitiringkupai waringka. Ka ngananya waru kutjara tjunkupai. Ka nganana ngarala nganytjilpai kilinarira wiyaringkula. Nikiti tjuta nganana nyinangi iriti. Mr Trudingerla paluru teacher nganampa.

Kuula panya nganampa pupanyi nyuntu nyangu tjuminta kutju panya ngaranyi. Mr Trudingernya kuulangka nyinangi nyara paluru nganampa teacher kala kuula nyara palula nyinangi tjuminta kutju panya ngaranyi wali panya top houseala itingka.

What did they teach you at school? Reading and writing and math?

Uwa, ngurpa nganana mukuringangi munu nganana nintiringangi kuulangka.

Munu walka tjuta palyaningi?

Munu nganana paintamilaningi tjitji uwankarangku.

were happy living on kangaroo meat. So I was a baby when my parents brought me to Ernabella, where I grew up. We didn't have much food there: the rations were only small as the missionaries had just started to distribute them. So we took the small rations. The older children fetched them.

I had grown into a young girl then and I went to school with all the other children I had grown up with and Dr Duguid was our first teacher.** We had cow and goat milk. An Anangu house worker milked the goats early in the morning and she carried the milk in a bucket over to the missionary's house. People gathered at the rocks, where the bridge next to the store is nowadays, to drink the milk and they made a fire and sat around it. We went to school early in the morning. Someone had lit a fire for us and everything was prepared: towels, combs, everything. We had showers under the cold water of the hose and all the children gathered around a big fire to warm up. In those days, we teenage boys and girls were naked. Mr Trudinger was our teacher.

The school used to be near the top house. There's only the cement foundation left next to where the preschool is now.

What did they teach you at school? Reading, writing and math?

We didn't know any of this, but we wanted to learn at school.

And what about painting?

We painted as well, all the children made drawings at school.

*** In fact Mr Trudinger was the first teacher.*

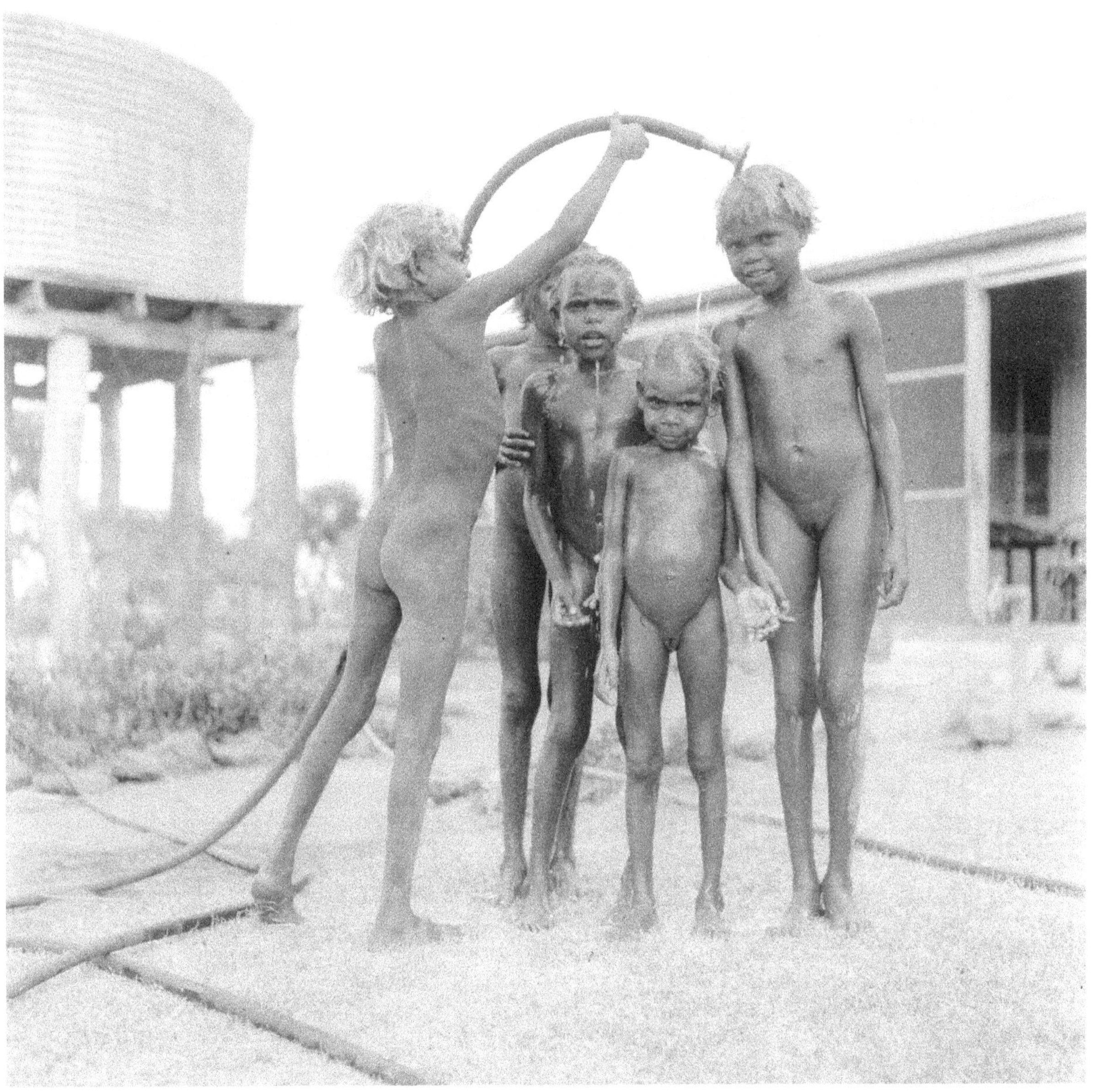

And what did the children draw?

Walka munu lita kulu kulula walkatjunangi uwankara kutjupa kutjupa tjuta. Dr Duguidalu ngananyanya nintiningi picturengka Ingkilitja wiya, only Pitjantjatjara nganana wangkapai munu walkatjunkupai miru panya munu tarka palunyalanya nintiningi Ingkilitjangku nintintja wiyangku

And what did the children draw?

We drew designs and wrote letters, we did all kinds of things. Dr Duguid used pictures because we didn't speak English, but only Pitjantjatjara.

Where did he learn Pitjantjatjara?

He learnt Pitjantjatjara at school: the children taught him our language

Children showering under the hose, 1951 (smallest child, Yangkuyi Yakiti, child holding hose probably Nungalka Stanley) (photograph Richard Seeger collection XP 1105, courtesy Museum of Victoria)

Dr Duguidalu Pitjantjatjara kutju wangkangi ka paluru ngapartji tjananya nintinu Pitjantjatjaraku.

Where did he learn Pitjantjatjara?

Wiya, palunya anangu tjutangku nintinu Pitjantjatjaraku, walkatjura panya paluru nintiringu Pitjantjatjaraku munu paluru ninti alatjitu nyinapai. Tjitji tjutangku kungkawara tjutangku nintilpai palunya rawangku ka paluru nganana nyinara pukulpa nyinapai munula tjitji pulkaringulta.

Munula Mr Trudingerlakutu ankupai ka ngananananya mai ration ungkupai waluparangku flour sugar panya brown one munu blanket kutju panya tjipinyunguru palyantja Cameron blanket. Nganana mai ngalkula kuulangka tjarpapai mai tjukutjukutjarala nyinangi rice porridge kutjula ngalkupai mungawinki. Munula dinnerangka rice ngalkupai mungartji kutjupala ngalkupai tjukutjuku kuka tjukutjuku.

And did you really want this, did you need this food? Did you get some kangaroo, or ngintaka or some maku?

Uwa, nganana makuku mukuringkupai munula ngalkupai rawangku munu nganana mai kampurarpa, wirinywirinypa, wangunu munu kunakanti palunya tjananya rungkara ngalkulpai kamingkulanya ungkupai ngunytjungku kulu kulu kala mai nyanga palunya ngalkula kunpu nyinapai pika wiya wankaru.

Munu nganana tjurtjungka tjarpapai choirku kalanya nintilpai Mr Trudingerlu kala nintiringulta munula kulilpai katutjangku nintilpai ngananananya uwankara. Kala katutjaku

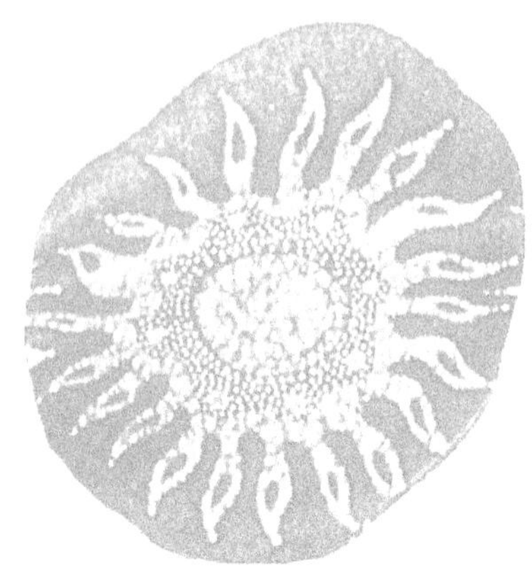

and he taught us to write 'm-i-r-u' and 't-a-r-k-a'. So, Anangu taught him Pitjantjatjara. Write this down: he learnt Pitjantjatjara from us and he taught us to write our language! The children and young girls constantly taught him. He was happy with this and we became big children.

And we went to Mr Trudinger and he gave us rations. A white woman distributed flour, brown sugar and one woollen blanket, a Cameron blanket. After breakfast, we went to school. We only had a small feed, just rice and porridge in the morning. And we ate rice for dinner and in the evening we ate a little bit of meat.

And did you really want this, did you need this food? Did you get some kangaroo, or ngintaka or some maku?

We also had our food: maku, kampurarpa, wirinywirinypa, wangunu and kunakanti. The seeds were ground to prepare a meal and our grandmothers and mothers fed us. This food is very healthy and you don't get ill.

We started a church choir with Mr Trudinger and God showed us the way, everything about Christianity. We learnt about Jesus and God in song

nintiringu Jesusaku inma inkantjikitja munu paluru ngananany a baptisealta katingu tjurtju nyara palula paluru ngananala tjulpinytja nintilpai tjurtju panya palangka panya pupanyi. Kala tjitji kulunypa tjuta tjarpapai Sunday munu tjukurpa kulilpai Mr Trudingerlu pula Nyingutaku mitangku wangkanyangka ka paluru ngayuku kulypalpa paluru nganana tjitji kulunypa tjuta nintiringkupai nganmanypa.

Ka paluru yangupala munu wati nyanga paluru tjana tjukurtjara tjutangku kulinu munta uwa tjipila mantjila munula shepherd tjuta tjura tjipi tjuta kanyintjaku Anapalala, buluka wiyangka. Munu tjana mantjinu tjipi tjuta munu tjunu Anapalala ngura winkinka Youngs Well Donald Well, Black Hill, Tjatjala ka tjipi tjutalta ngarangi. Ka shepherd tjuta anangu tjuta nyinangi iriti ka ration palunya tjana katira ungangi first shepherd. Mr Bennettalu Walterlu pula tjananya ungkupai Walternya Mr Bennettaku warka palyalpai paluru ngayuku kuta munu paluru tjana ungkupai mai panya ration tjipi tjara tjuta munu para ungkula mungartji kutju wirkankupai ka shearing shed ngarangi tjipi panya shearamilalpai kaya wati tjutangku nyara palula shearmilalpai.

What were the women doing?

Ka tjana minyma tjutangku inyu rungkalpai, spinning ka wali tjukutjuku ngarangi nganampa inyu rungkalpai wali craftroom tjukutjuku kala tjitji pulkaringkula palulanguru kulilpairingu munu nganana ipi tjararingu. Ka wati tjutangku

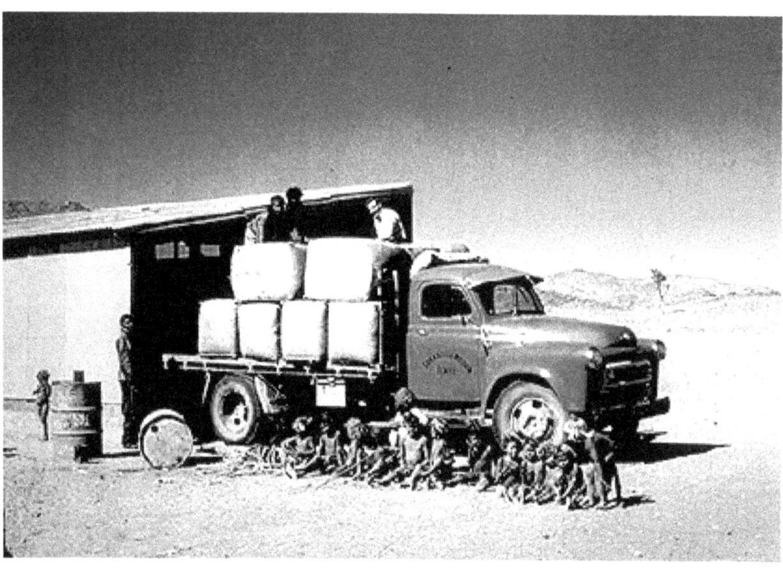

The wool truck, 1958, with Bill Elliott sitting on top of the bails of wool (photograph Reverend Bruce Edenborough collection #9563, courtesy Pitjantjatjara Council)

and praying and we were baptised in church. That was the brush shelter where we had been taught. The young children went to church on Sunday to listen to the word and the gospel. Mr Trudinger and Nyinguta's husband – that's my uncle and I went to school with him – were praying and teaching and he became a church leader after he had finished school.

And the missionaries decided to have sheep at Ernabella, but not cattle. They established sheep camps at the bores and Anangu were shepherding. So they bought the sheep and brought them to Ernabella to all the bores: Youngs Well, Donalds Well, Black Hill and Tjatja. So there were lots of sheep to be minded and the main shepherd, Mr Bennett, and my brother Walter, who worked with him, gave rations to the shepherds. They went out to the sheep camps and came back to Ernabella in the afternoon.

What were the women doing?

shearamilalpai munu Bedfordangka loada katipai Finkealakutu munu trainangka iyalpai Adelaidealakutu pulangkita tjuta palyantjaku. Ka palyara nganampa iyalpai pulangkita palunya ka piranpa tjutangku mantjilpai pulangkita wiru tjuta munu ngananganya ungkupai kuulitja tjuta.

Ka nganana wiltja wirungka nyinapai wali wiya. Ka hospital tjukutjuku ngarangi ka sister kutju nyinangi munu ngananganya alpamilaningi munu anangu tjuta iyalpai Flying Doctorngka. Ka nganana nyinapai kalanya sister kutjungku kanyilpai kala pukulpa nyinapai pikatjara ka irapulaina pitjapai Alice Springsalanguru miritjinatjara munu wanipai pika panya measle ngaranyangka ka nganana tjitji pulkalta nyinangi warka ninti.

Ka tjinguru wati paluru tjana ritiringkula bomb waninyangka measle pulka pakanu nyara (Maralingkala) tjangati ka puyu pitjangu ka nganana tjitji pulkangku nyangangi kaya pika pulka ngaringi ngaltutjara anangu tjuta. Panya measletjara paluru tjana pika pulkaringu. Ngura ini Emunya pungu nyara palulaya bombatjunu ka Mr Bakerlu wangkara wantikatingu, nyura kulinma panya tjana bomb tjunanyi kuwari nyarangka. Ka Mr MacDougall palumpa malpa tjutatjara ngura panya Woomeralakutu anu anangu kutjupa tjutakulu katingu. Ka nganana palulanguru kuliningi kuwari kunyu bombatjunanyi munula nyinara nyinara mulapatu kulinu bomb waninyangka ulparira. Emunya pungu paluru aputjara ka puyu panya Anapalala wirkanu munu wirkara ngananganya tjutunu kala nganana pika pulkatjararingu palulanguru.

There was a shearing shed where Anangu men sheared the sheep. And the women spun wool in the small craft shed that was made for the spinners. We grew up into big girls and learnt all these things. And after the shearing the men loaded the wool on the Bedford truck and drove to Finke, where it was put on the train to Adelaide. We received blankets in return from down south. The missionaries gave beautiful blankets to the schoolchildren.

And we were living in bush huts, not in houses. There was a little hospital with one sister to help us and the Flying Doctors. The plane came in from Alice Springs bringing medicine, and those who had fallen ill with measles were glad. During the measles epidemic, the medicine was dropped from the plane. That's when I was a working girl.

When the white men were ready, they dropped the bomb on this side from Maralinga and severe measles broke out. The smoke came when I was a big girl, and we were all lying down in great pain. Those who were affected suffered badly, the poor things. The bomb exploded at Emu and Mr Baker told us that we needed to know that bombs were being tested. And Mr MacDougall took his friends, the traditional owners, to Woomera to discuss the matter. And they learnt from him what was going on. They waited to hear the bomb and, after a while, they heard it exploding in the south. The bomb was ignited at Emu, but the smoke shifted towards Ernabella and covered the whole place like a cloud. We became very sick, measles broke out and we got chickenpox from the

Measles bombanguru utiringu ka puyu panya Anapalala wirkanu puyu kura ka paluru tjana pika pulkatjararingu. Anapalala wirkanu puyu paluru panya nyuntu puyuku ninti? Paluru alatji pakanu munu Anapalanya tjutunu bomba waninyangka ka uwankara pikatjararingu urkalytjararingu chickenpoxanguru. Chickenpox panya purtju purunypa pulka pakanu ka uwankara miri red pulkaringu. Pika pulka, uwa, 1000, wampa or 2000 tjinguru ngayulu ngurpa. Uwa winki ilungu ngura kutjupanguru, Utjulanguru ilungu Mimilila tjanala munkaranguru wiyaringu nyara Witjintitjala tjanala tjuta mulapa winki wiyaringu measlenguru bombangku wiyanu kutjupa wilurara tjutatu ilungu ngura nyangangka ilungu Utjulanguru. Ka ma ngarira wanara nyangangi miri tjuta ma ngarira waninyangka urilta. Ka Anapala cemetery winki ngaranyi nganana tjunutjunkuntja tjunutjunkuntja tjuta winki mulapa. Mrs Bennettanyala alpamilaningi ka kutjupa tjuta church panya tjulpinytja unngu ngaringi ka kutjupa tjuta karungka ngaringi panya wati ngarira wananingiya rutangka officewanu hospital irititjawanu panya winki ngaringi pikatjara tjuta. Ka munga nyara palula nganana tjitji mankurpa wanka nyinangi – ngayulu Peter Nyaningunya tjitji pulka Ingkantjinya paluru nganana munu nganaku Kunipauku ngunytju panya minyma panya palatja paluru nganana panya paluru ngali kungka kutjara ka tjana nyitayira mankurpa Mr Trudingerku roomangkala nganana ngaripai pikatjara tjuta ka tjana pikatjara winki anangu winki ka tjara ilungi mungangka tjurtju nyangangka nganampa kami tjuta

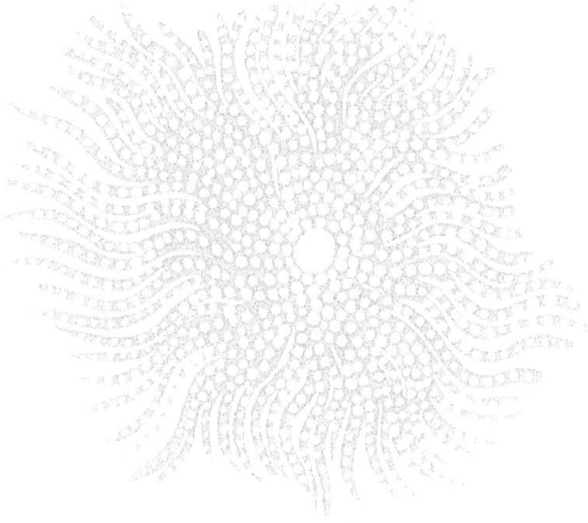

bomb. When the dangerous smoke came to Ernabella, we fell very very ill. Have you heard about all this? That's how it happened: the smoke covered Ernabella when it was tested at Emu and everyone got sick with flu, chickenpox, scabies – our skin was burning red. Many people were affected, 1000, maybe 2000, I'm not sure. A lot of people died who were from Areyonga, from beyond Mimili and some from Witjintitjala [Granite Downs]. They died from these measles, from that bomb. And people from the west died as well, so many passed away. Some were from Utju; they died in Ernabella. Bodies were lying everywhere, some already dead, others dying. And each day people were buried in the cemetery in Ernabella and we were helping Mrs Bennett. Some were lying in the church, some in the creekbed, and on the road near the hospital where the office used to be, everywhere. And that night, three children were still healthy, and they looked after the ill: myself, Peter Nyaningu and Ingkatji, who was a big boy. We and Kunipa's mother, that is we two girls and three

tjamu tjuta kulypalpa tjuta tjurtjungka tjulypinypangka itingka.

Uwa nyanga palulanguru wiyaringu.

young boys, were sleeping in Mr Trudinger's room. Some people died that night in the church, and our grandmothers, grandfathers and uncles died beside the church.

That's the end of the story.

A note on historical data

In 1985 there was a royal commission into the British atomic bomb tests at Emu (257 kilometres to the southeast of Ernabella) in 1953 and Maralinga (420 kilometres to the south) in 1956–57, but possible effects on the health of the residents at Ernabella have not been ascertained.

Winifred Hilliard, who worked in Ernabella as the art and craft adviser between 1954 and 1986, but who was on leave during 1957 and thus was probably not in the area at the time of the Maralinga bomb tests, reports that she never heard of the explosions having been seen or heard in the community, nor of the fallout threatening the area around the southwestern end of the Musgrave Ranges. This is the part of the ranges to which Nura Rupert refers in her story when she mentions that people out west were dying as well. Hilliard says that the ranges themselves, including Ernabella, were not within the zone of the nuclear fallout from the explosions at Emu. To her knowledge, 'the black cloud was seen at cattle stations southeast of Ernabella', that is, outside the Musgrave Ranges and north of Emu.

One of the eyewitnesses to, and victims of, the tests, Lallie Lennon, describes her horrific experience when she was in Mintabie, only 150 kilometres south of Ernabella, in Adele Pring's Women of the Centre *(Pascoe Publishing 1990). She tells of her and her children's suffering from burning red skin, vomiting and dysentery and not knowing at that time that they were affected by radioactive dust. Like Nura Rupert, she depicts the symptoms in terms of known diseases, such as flu, chickenpox and scabies.*

She also mentions MacDougall, the 'native patrol' officer for the Woomera rocket range, as one of the few white people trying to help. Epidemics documented for Ernabella are measles in 1948 and 1956–57, and chickenpox in 1954–55.

3

about mission times
missionary tjuta pitjanytja ara

FIRST MISSIONARY COMING
WATI PIRANPA KUWARIPATJARA PITJANYTJA

(Translations by Kanytjupai Armstrong)

Alec Minutjukur

So the mission started here, and we come and go, walk, we didn't stay here. They started school – Ron Trudinger was the first teacher – but the children were not wearing clothes, because maybe they get sick, pika. I think it is a good idea, no clothes – old ways, old days.

Ka piranpa nyinakatinyangka walingka kutju nganana nyinanytja wiya para ngarapai munula ankula maluku pitjapai mulamula nyinanytja wiya kaya kuula tjunu nganampa ka Ron Trudingernya nganampa nintilpai nyinangi kuwaripatjara paluru warara ka nyara palula ara tjitji tjutangku mantara kanyintja wiya nikiti uwankara nyinapai. Tjinguru pikatjararingkunytjakutawara nyanga alatji ngarangi wiru mulapa.

Margaret Dagg

Mission time wiru. They were teaching us, discipline, ninti pulka. Always on time to work. Now, people are lazy.

Iritiyanku missionary nyinanytja arangka wiru mulapa ngarangi kalanya piranpa tjutangku pulkara mulapa nintilpai kala mungamunga pitjapai munula rawa warkaripai wirura mulapa ka malatja tjuta kuwari pakuringanyi.

Tjikalyi Tjapiya

Ngananala naked nyinapai kuulangka – no clothes at school. When we finish our school, somebody made a dress for us, special. And then I put on the new dress and now I'm a young kungka.

Nganana iriti nikiti nyinangi kuulangka mantara wiya ka kuula wiyaringkunyangka kutjupangku nganampa tiritja palyanu wiru mulapa munu ngananamya tjarpatjunu kana kuwaripatu nyanga pamparingku wiya nyinanyi.

Wally Dunn

When first missionary coming, the people been sitting: no car, no rifle. [Instead] spear and woomera, and really interesting work Anangu way. When white fella coming up, big changes. The missionary shooting dog, dingo, and selling and giving tucker, clothes, everything. The missionary looking after Ernabella mission.*

And people from Pipalyatjara, different place, is coming up from west to Ernabella, towards us, start grow up a community.

Wati piranpa mankurpa nguwanpa nganmanyitja nyinangi ka anangu tjuta mutuka raipula kulu kanyintja wiya kulatatjara kalitjara kutju nyinangi wiru mulapa ngarangi nganmanypa anangu tjutaku. Ka piranpa tjuta pitjanyangka kutjuparingu pulkara alatjitu palu wati piranpa tjutangku iriti papa inura tjuta paura tjalamilaningi munuya mai mantjira mantara kulu kulu ngananamya ungangi munuya wati mitjiniri tjutangku ngura nyanga Anapalanya wirura atunymara kanyilpai.*

Kaya anangu kutjupa tjuta ngura Pipalyatjaralanguru pitjangu wiluraranguru kala tjunguringkula ngura pulka palyanu.

Ernabella mission station, early 1960s (photograph Lou Borgelt collection #4263, courtesy Pitjantjatjara Council)

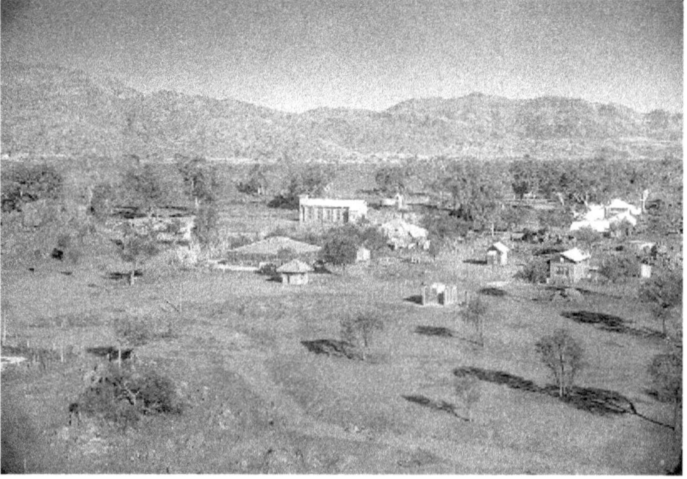

** The narrator probably uses the same term for both doggers and missionaries, translated in Pitjantjatjara as 'white man'.*

THE OLD ERNABELLA
ANAPALA IRITITJA

Peter Nyaningu

(Translation by Kanytjupai Armstrong)

1. Homeland office today. First it was Mr Love's house, and then Mr Trudinger's first place.
2. The first community office
3. Church
4. Vestry
5. The Bennetts' place. It was pushed down and only the foundation remains.
6. 'The Oleanders' [named after the trees growing in the garden], where the main shepherd stopped. That's Mr Ward and Mr Elliott. Then it became kungka tjutaku house, for teachers and nurses. That's where the match-making happened among the white fellas.

1. Kuwari Anilayaku uputju ngarinyi palu nganmanypa Mr Loveku wali ngaringi ka mala Mr Trudingerkuringu.
2. Uputju nyara paluru tjaataringu anangukuringkula
3. Church
4. Wati tjukurtjaraku ruma
5. Bennettaku ngura panya untura punkatjinganu ka puluwa kutju uti ngarinyi.
6. Nganmanypa Oliandernya tjipi atunymankupai tjutaku ngura ngarangi Mr Wardaku Mr Elliottku pulampa munu palula mala kungkawara tjutakuringu nintilpai tjutaku munu nurse tjuta ngura.

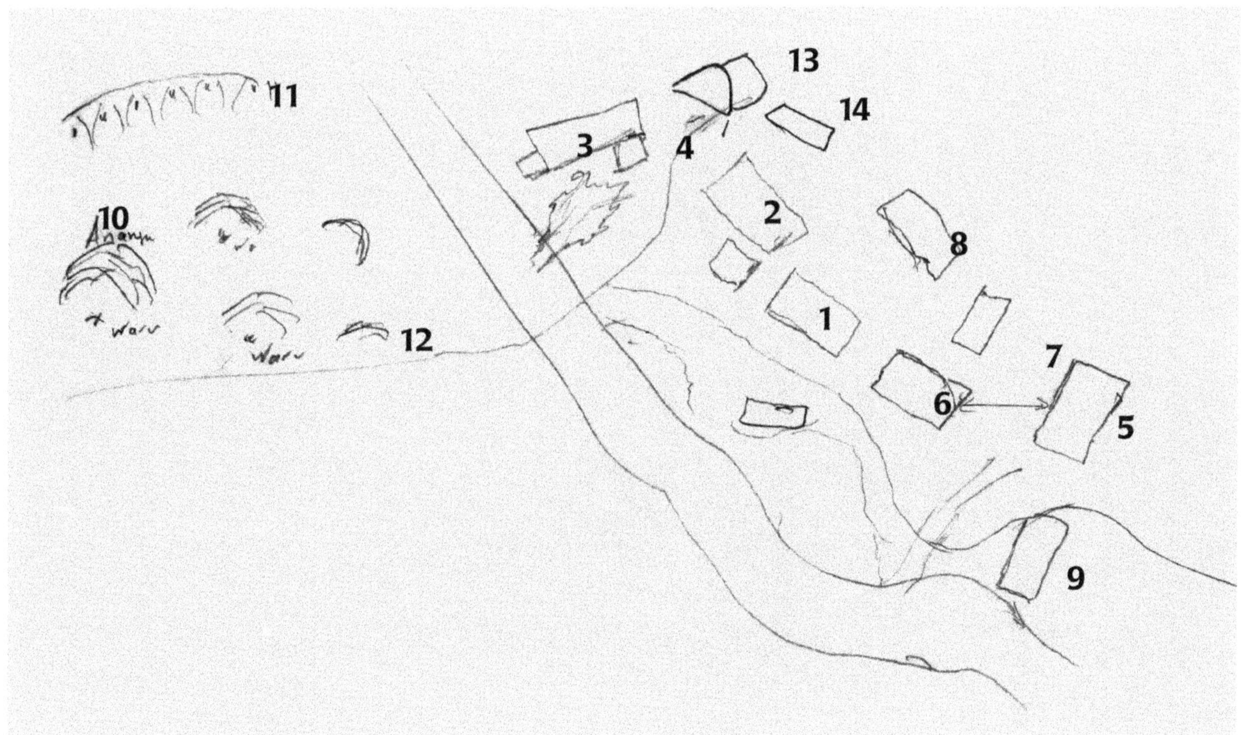

Ernabella in mission times, by Peter Nyaningu, pencil on paper, 1996 (Ute Eickelkamp collection)

Thus at first it was the white fellas' place.

7. Miss Hilliard's craftroom
8. New house, the store manager's
9. Ms Elliott's and Mrs Bennett's house. When Mrs Bennett [her name was Turvey then] married, they moved to the old wati's place.
10. Anangu's place
11. Young men's camp
12. Young women's camp
13. Bakery. Iwana's and Yuminiya Ken's mother worked there.
14. The store. Food was given to Anangu by white people. The women eat back at camp, some men sat with older men next to the store because that was the big rule: young men and women stay separate! Older men shout out clearly, 'Mapitja! Ara!', 'Go away! Get out!'

The mothers looked after their sons who were staying at a distance, brought tea halfway, which the sons picked up, morning and supper.

All day, son is working out bush getting malu. His little brother takes it from him and gives it to the parents in return for water.

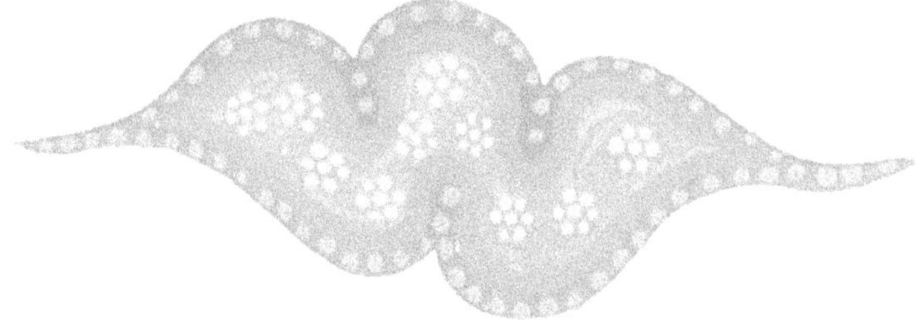

Alatjiya nganmanypa ngarangi piranpa tjutaku ngura.

7. Miss Hilliardanya craftroomaku mayatja nyinangi
8. Panya kuwari tjuwa kanyilpaiku wali ngaranyi
9. Ms Elliottaku Mrs Bennettaku pulampa wali panya [paluru nganmanypa Miss Turveynya] nyinangi munu Bennettlu altinyangka pula anu wati tjutaku wali irititjakutu.
10. Anangu tjutaku ngura
11. Wati wanngu tjutaku ngura
12. Kungkawara tjutaku ngura
13. Mai paulpai Iwanaku pulampa Yuminiya Kenku ngunytjungku pula.
14. Tjuwa mai kulu kululampa palyanu piranpa tjutangku ka minyma tjutangku mai ngurangka ngalkupai ka wati wanngu tjuta wati pulka tjutangka nyinapai tjuwangka itingka panya nyanga paluru tjanampa ara kaya wati wanngu kungkawara tjuta mauntalpa patu patu nyinapai tjungu wiya panya wati tjilpi tjutangku tjananya ilaringkunyangka nyakula mirara pailpai patu nyinanytjaku kaya wati tjukutjuku tjuta patu nyinapai.

Ngunytjungka kurungka kaya iruwa mai katira tjunkupai ngunytju tjutangku kala pakara mantjilpai tjunkula ankunyangka mungawinki.

Mungartji tjintu kutjupa tjintu kutjupa munu katja tjuta nintiringkupai patu nyinara malu wakantjaku munuya katira ungkupai tjitji tjuta ngunytju mama ungkunytjaku minakitjangku.

A DAY IN MISSION TIMES
TJINTU MISSIONARY NYINANYTJA ARA

Tjikalyi Tjapiya
(Translation by Kanytjupai Armstrong)

I got a job in the house: cleaning, washed the walls, the floor, scrubbing. Big job, that one. White fella tjuta, they leave the house in the morning, go to work, and we look after that baby.

The girls make wiltja and milpatjunanyi, sitting down and telling her own story. And games, make wiltjas like a woman. Our mothers sitting around making mai, kuka, everything. And children plays here, close to their mothers.

The young girls sit around in the big shade of a tree and sleep

Ngayuluna warkaripai walingka mununa wali para paltjipai wallpa mununa puluwa pulkara rungkalpai warka pulkana palyapai. Anangu piranpaku ngurangka tjana panya ngarira tjinturingkula ankupai warkaku kala nganana tjanampa tjitji tjuta atunymara kanyilpai.

Minyma tjutangku wiltja pulka palyapai nyinakatira milpatjura tjukurpa wangkapai kala para nyinara arintara kulilpai paluru wangkanyangka munula game tjutaku kulu inkapai munu minyma

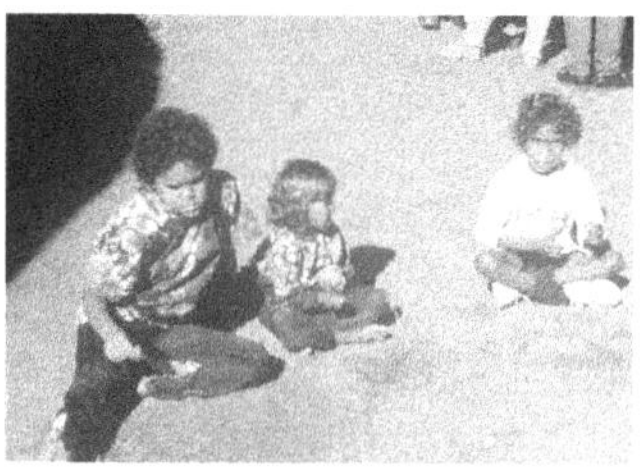

Suzanne and Tanya Kunmanara, Laurabell Kunmanara (left to right), 1996 (photograph Ute Eickelkamp)

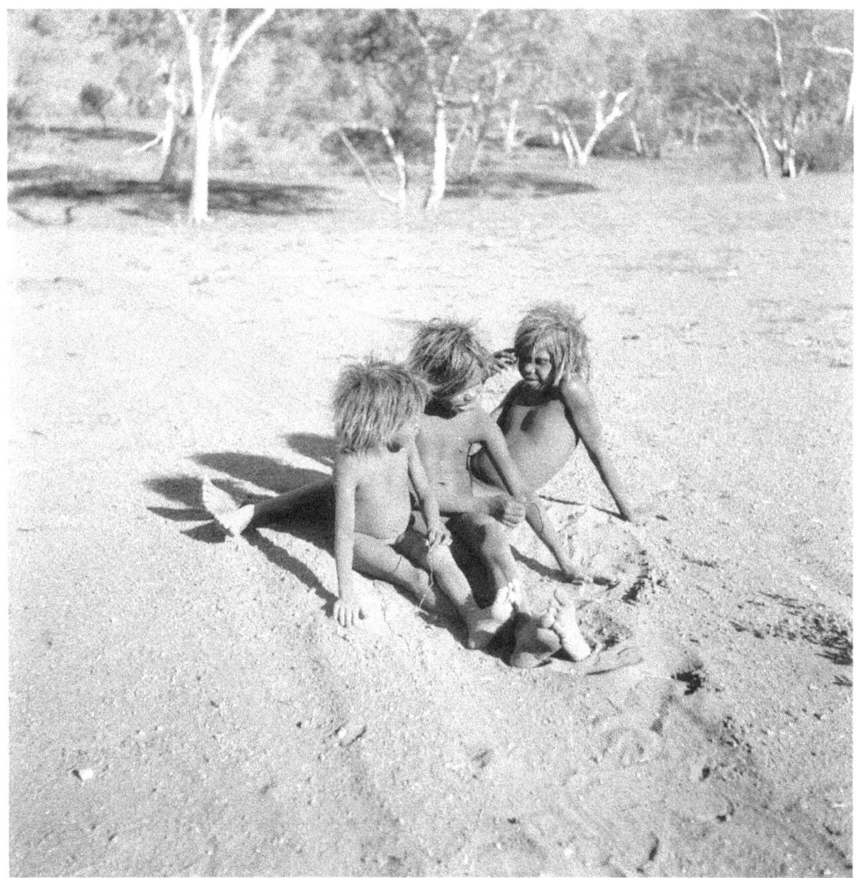

Young girls playing the sand storytelling game in a creekbed, 1951 (photograph Richard Seeger collection XP 475, courtesy Museum of Victoria)

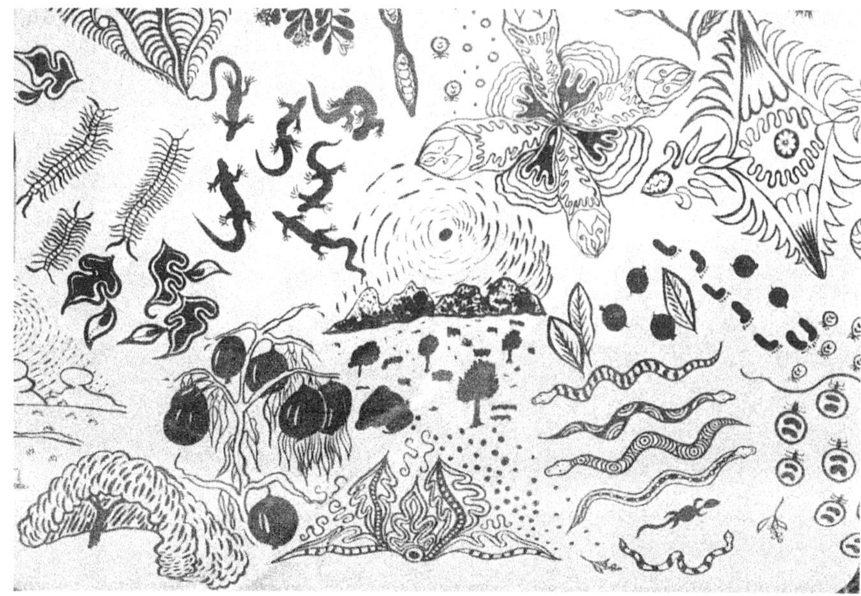

Home/Nguratjara, collective work, printed by Marie Warren, screenprint on fabric, late 1980s or early 1990s (Ernabella Arts collection, photograph Ernabella Arts)

sometimes. And after sleep, we go out on a donkey, go right away from Ernabella. You can catch rabbit and tinka, and bush-berries, bush-tomatoes, bush-onions.

And fathers go hunting.

We've been learning our way too.

When we come back we saw that, 'Ah, damper is waiting for me, tea, mother made for me'.

Wiltja, make fire inside. We sleep: father, mother, tjitji. When we big kid, we'd stay with our sisters' wiltja, young girls' house separate one. And our brothers stay away from us. And the big brothers and tjamus look after them.

Yangkuyi Yakiti extracting witchetty grubs from shrub root, 1995 (photograph Ute Eickelkamp)

minymangku wiltja palyara inkapai ka nganampa ngunytju tjutangku mai kuka kulu paulpai ngurangka kala ngurangka itingka ilatu ngarala inkapai.

Kaya kungka tjuta punu wiltjangka nyinapai munuya kutjupa ara kunkunaripai munula kunkuntjanu pakara donkeyingka tatira ankupai parari mulapa Anapalalanguru rapitaku tinkaku kampurarpaku tawal-tawalpaku kulu munu tjanmataku kulu.

Munula mamanya ngunytjunya tjananya kulu nyakula nintiringkupai.

Kala malaku pitjala nyakupai mai tampa nganmanytju paura tjunkunytja ngarinyi ngayuku, ngunytjulutju tjunukupai.

Wiltja mamalu pula ngunytulu palyalpai munulanya unngu tjunkupai munula tjungu ngaripai kala kunkawara tjut wali walytjangka mauntalpa ngaripai ka kutanya tjana ngananala ilaringkupai wiya ngananala ka nganampa kuta pulka tjuta tjamulu kanyilpai.

'PUTTING THE STICK DOWN'
MILPATJUNANYI, A GREAT STORYTELLING TRADITION

Ute Eickelkamp

I look at this 'game', played mostly by young girls, as a kind of performing news magazine or a puppet play: stories about daily events, memorable past incidents and 'teaching dramas' are depicted in the sand using a bent stick or, nowadays, a piece of wire and eucalypt leaves.

The leaves feature as characters of the narration with the larger ones representing adults, a bent leaf for a female and a flat leaf for a male, while smaller leaves represent children. The characters are laid out on the smoothed surface of the sand – reminiscent of a theatre stage – and the performance begins with the storyteller beating the stick on the ground with one hand, creating a rhythm to accompany the narration, while with the other hand she arranges anew the choreography for each scene, after the surface has been cleared again in a sweeping gesture.

The flow of gestures, in contrast to the compelling, yet steady, rhythmic beat binding the sequences together, creates the formal frame of the story performance, which can develop into a highly dramatic piece.

The punishment of a young unmarried couple for having sneaked out bush at night-time, for example, forms the culminating end of a story. The man is speared by piercing a stick through the leaf, and the young woman beaten by hitting and crushing the leaf, with the narrator calling out at the top of her voice, the rhythm speeding up, leaving the performance ground in a wild mess.

Narrator and characters become one in such a lively performance, which can hardly be captured on paper, but Yangkuyi Yakiti illustrated a few scenes for the sake of documenting this important element of women's visual-narrative tradition. Another type of sand storytelling game involves graphic signs drawn in the sand instead of using leaves. The sand graphs depict places, travel routes, features of the landscape, or animal tracks. This version of the game is not represented here.

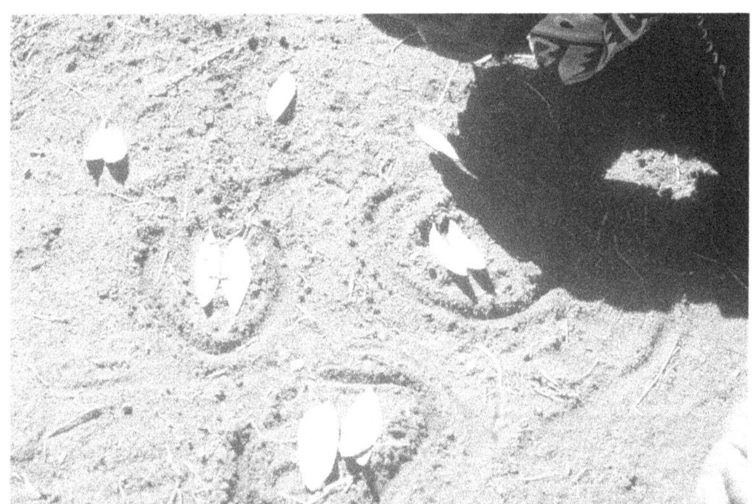

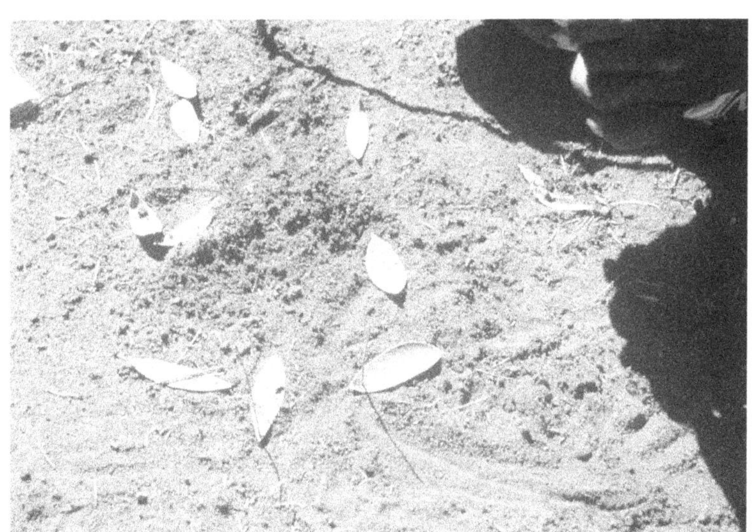

Demonstration of the sand storytelling game with eucalypt leaves by Nungalka Stanley, 1996 (photograph Ute Eickelkamp)

While leaves (nyalpi) feature in contemporary artworks, the iconographic elements of the sand storytelling games have not been transferred to works of Ernabella designs in introduced media. Rather, one could speak of a continuity of aesthetics and techniques: the beating of the stick in the sand might be compared to the canting with which wax is applied on to a length of batik, a medium with lenient qualities similar to sand. The sweeping flow of gestures accompanying the storytelling games can be observed in the execution of the Ernabella design, which is sometimes drawn in the sand as well, ever since the craftroom women developed it into a tradition of its own.

Yangkuyi Yakiti
(Translation by Ute Eickelkamp)

Children play the sand storytelling game. The leaves represent a young couple [minyma wati], a father, mother and child [mama, ngunytju, tjitji] and a group of young women [kungkawara tjuta].

After school [schoolangka malangka], they go out bush, riding donkeys [angkupai tangkiyika] to collect bush-tomatoes [kampurarpa], and figs [ili], witchetty grubs [maku], honeyants [tjala].

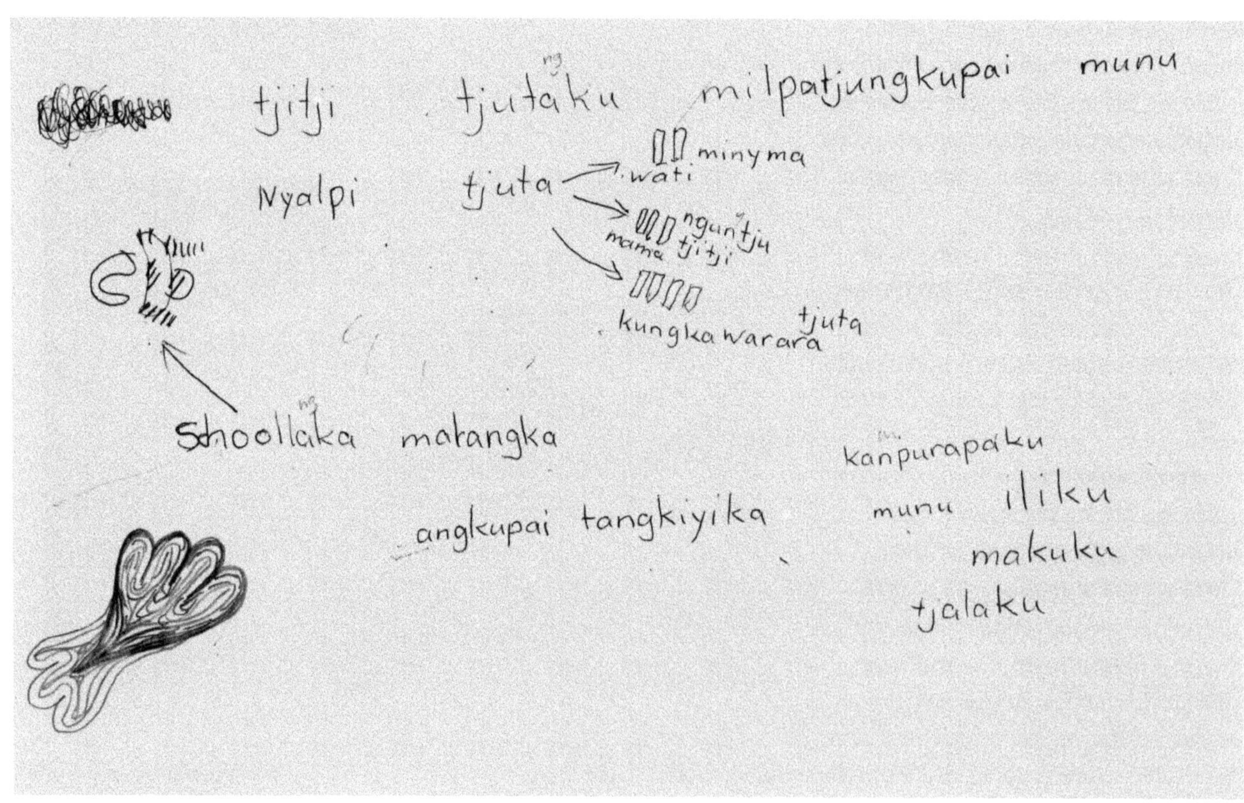

The sand storytelling game, by Yangkuyi Yakiti, ballpoint pen on paper, 1996
(Ute Eickelkamp collection)

WE HAD NO MONEY BUT GOOD WORK
MANI WIYA PALU WARKA WIRU

At Yangkuyi's – Yangkuyiku wiltjangka

Yangkuyi Yakiti

(Translation by Ute Eickelkamp)

Nganana iriti wiltjangka nyinangi mamanya munu ngunytjunya nganana ka mamalu palyalpai kulata miru ka ngunytjulu wool rungkalpai munu rungkara wiyaringkula katira tjalamilapai manikitjangku munu mantjira mai payamilalpai.

I used to live in a bush hut with my parents, and my father was making spears and spearthrowers while mother was spinning wool. She would take the spun wool (to the craftroom or the mission) and get money for it to pay for food.

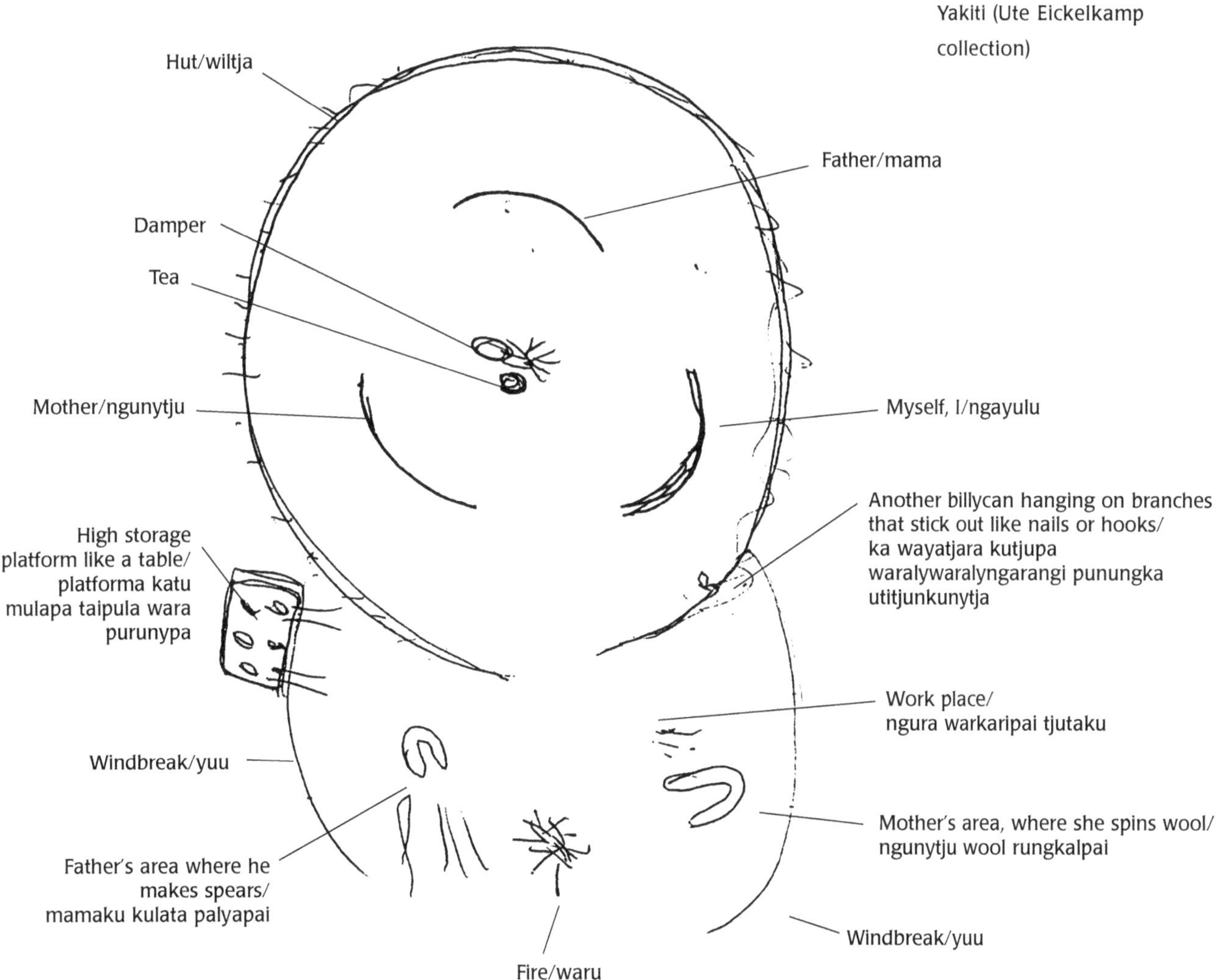

A family bush hut, by Yangkuyi Yakiti (Ute Eickelkamp collection)

All that work – Wark nyanga pulka

Alison Curley, Kunmanara Brumby and Nura Ward

(Translation by Kanytjupai Armstrong)

The young girls washed wool by hand. It came from the sheep that were shepherded by two couples at Youngs Well, Kunma Piti, Balfour Well, Womikata and other places while their children were at school. Most of these old sheep camps are homelands now.

The women made jam from a white fruit like a melon, and Topsy made quandong jam. Other women were cooking and making bread in the bakery. The mission had goats, which were milked by Nura Rupert's parents every morning.

Rations were taken out on the only car the mission had, the green 'Lucy truck'.

On Mondays, rations were taken to Itjinpiri, Youngs Well, Womikata and Wintuwintu.

On Wednesdays, men collected firewood, carrying it on their heads.

On Thursdays, rations were brought to Kunma Piti, Gilpins Well,

Nganana kungkawara tjutangku tjipi inyu marangku paltjilpai panya anangu kurira kurirangkuya kutjarangku kutjarangku atunymara kanyilpai tjipi tjuta ngura ini nyanganta Tjalyiritjala Kunmapitila Balfour Wellala Womikatala munu ngura kutjupa tjutangka kulu ka tjitji tjuta kuulangka nyinapai. Panya nganana kuwari nyinanyi tjipi tjutaku ngurangka.

Minyma tjutangkuya jama palyalpai piranpa tjutangku nintinyangka mai panya melona nguru ka Topsylu wayanu nguru jama palyalpai. Kaya minyma kutjupa tjarangku mai purita paulpai ka nyara palula ara nanikuta ngarangitu ka Nura Rupertaku mama ngunytjungku atunymara kanyira milka mantjilpai tjintu kutjupa tjintu kutjupa rawangku.

Ka mai ratjina tjanampa katipai mutuka kutjungka mutuka paluru ini Lucynya walka ukiriukiri.

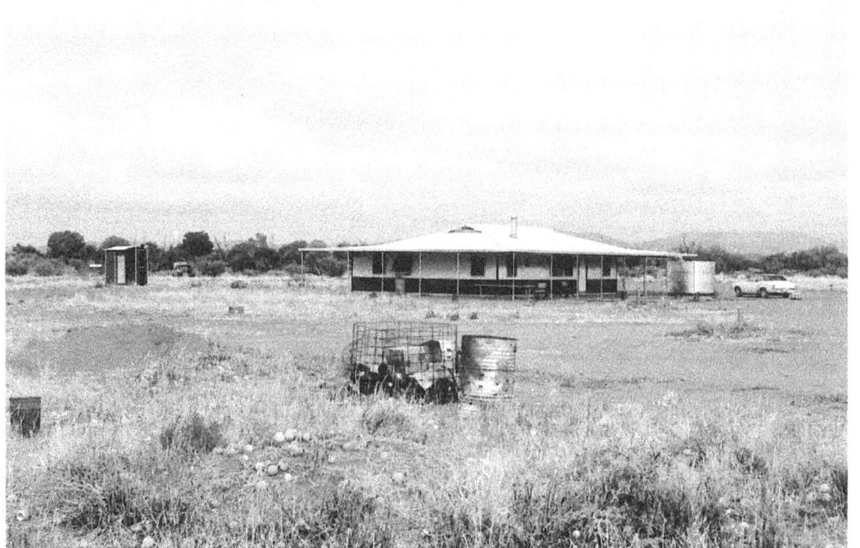

Kanytjupai Armstrong's homeland, Balfour Well, 1995 (photograph Ute Eickelkamp)

Tjiwuru, Tjatja and Balfour Well. They were taken on a cart pulled by two horses. That old cart is still sitting next to the craftroom.

For all that work no money, only two bob, or ten bob, only blankets and mai. Clothes wiya, no scabies, no boil, everybody clean.

On Saturday and Sunday, we go

Munu Monday ratjina katipai Itjinpirilakutu Tjalyiritjalakutu Womikatalakutu munu Wintuwintulakutu.

Ka Wednesdayngka wati tjutangku waru tjuta tjinangku ankula tjalira katipai katangku.

Ka Thursdayngka mai ratjina katipai Kunmapitilakutu Gilpins

Sheep camp, 1951 (Richard Seeger collection XP 41, courtesy Museum of Victoria)

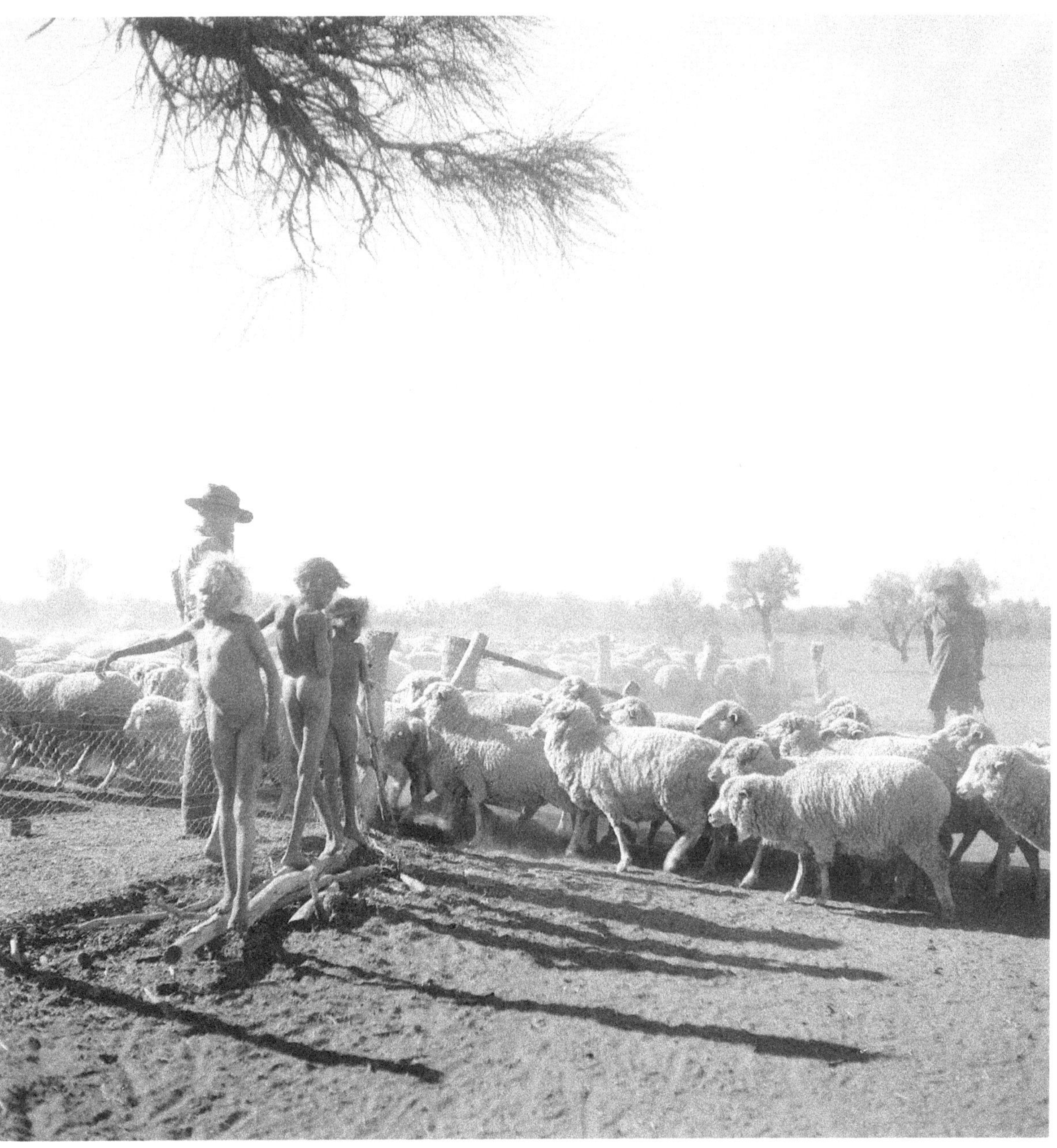

out with a donkey, take all the kids. After work on Saturday morning we get rations and go out bush.

Good times, but now . . . all the kids have radio, TV, staying inside, making that brain spin.

Wellalakutu Tjiwurulakutu Tjatjalakutu munu Balfour Wellalakutu. Tjanaya katipai wakinangka panya nyanytju kutjarangku ilara katipai panya wakina paluru kuwari nyinanyi craftroomangka itingka.

Nyara palula ara mani wiya two bob munu pulangkita mai kutju ngarangi tiritja tarawatja tjuta wiya kala purtju pika kunmanu wiya miri kilina alatjitiu nyinangi.

Munu Saturdayngka Sundayngka nganana ankupai tangkiyingka tjitji uwankara munula tjitji uwankara katipai parari mai ratjina mantjira puti kutu.

Nyara palula ara wiru mulapa ngarangi palu kuwari tjitji tjutangku kulini radio munu nyinara nyanganyi TV titutjarangku wali unngu kutju munuyanku ngukunypa kurani.

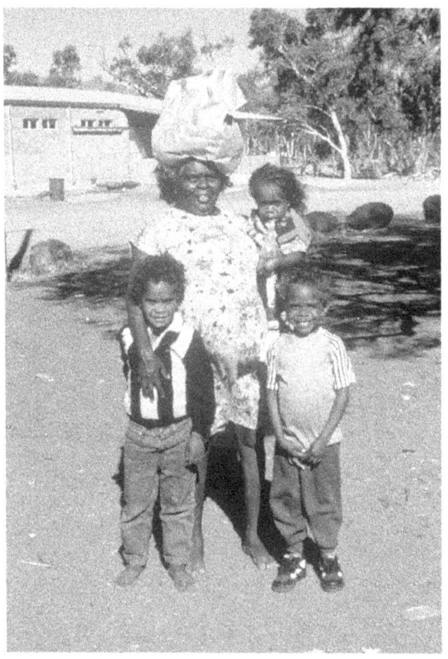

Tjunkaya Tapaya with Jangala (left), Glendon (right) and small girl, 1996 (photograph Ute Eickelkamp)

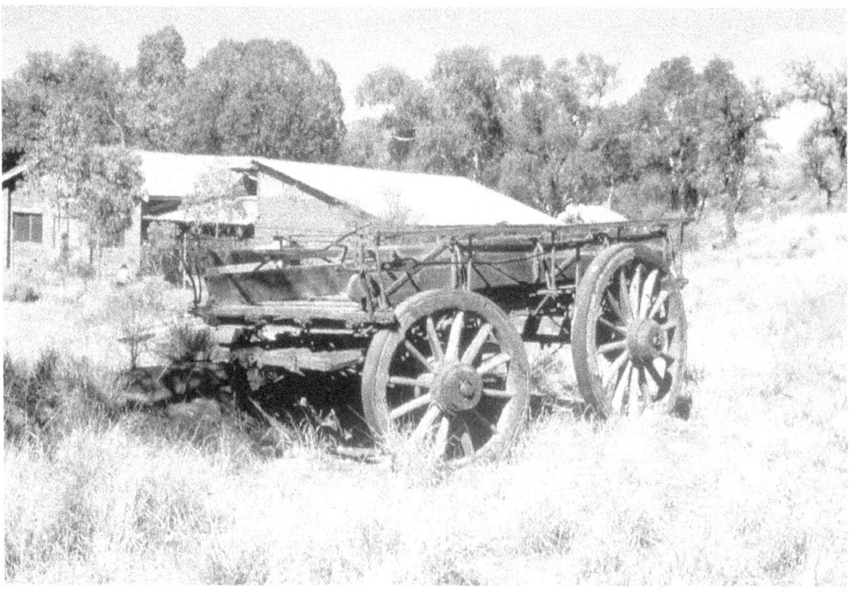

An old horse cart behind the craftroom, 1996 (photograph Ute Eickelkamp)

THINGS HAVE CHANGED
KUTJUPARINYTJA

(Translations by Kanytjupai Armstrong)

Alec Minutjukur

These days is bad, very bad. Old days, my day, pretty good. In mission days, keeping people to wash, clean, shower, wash blankets. They were giving us washing powder.

New days is very bad for people because everything come into community, like petrol sniffing, drinking, stealing, causing big community problem.

When I thinking back old day, I think it's the good old days.

Tjintu nyanga paluru tjana kuwari kura mulapa nyarakatinyi palu iriti ngayulu nyinanytja arangka wiru mulapa ngarangi. Mission dayangka nganana kilina nyinapai kalanya washing powder ungkupai pulangkita tjuta paltjintjaku.

Ka tjintu nyanga kuwari kura mulapa ngaranyi anangu kuraringkunyangka panya kuwari ngaranyi pitulu pantilpai tjuta waina tjikilpai kutitjunkupai kura pulka mulapa.

Kana malakutura kulini mulapayanku iriti wiru ngarangi.

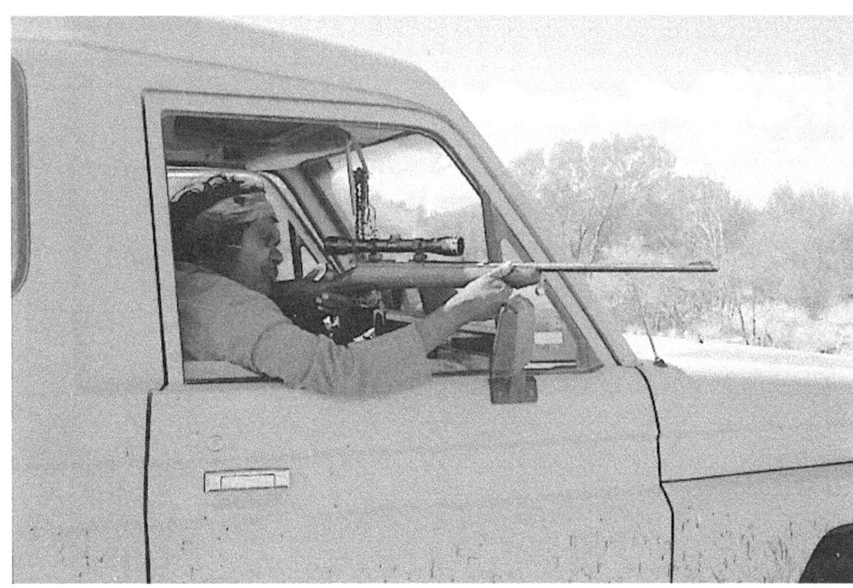

Pantjiti McKenzie shooting a kangaroo, 1995 (photograph Ute Eickelkamp)

Wally Dunn

Mission time is really hard for people . . . he like big boss, a little bit hard, but we changed to community now, to make it easy, uwa, our way.	Iriti wituwitu pulka ngarangi anangu tjutaku panya mayatja kutju nyinangi ka wituwitu ngarangi ka kuwari kampa kutjuparingu ka anangukuringkula palyaringu nguwanpa.
Still, we got Anangu way. We're teaching the young. With the young people he's grew up like white fella, he can't use the language, but we still stick to the language. Tjukurpa, we telling about that. Sometime, my granddaughter, grandson, I talk to them. I dancing sometime, I show them emu dancing, watersnake dancing. They learn from me watching, sometime singing.	Palu anangu tjuta palurutu nyinanyi kuwari munu nintini yangupala kungkawara tjuta kamiku tjamuku ara uwankara. Ka kutjupa tjuta piranpa tjutaku araku nintiringu munuya pulkaringanyi piranpa tjuta purunypa munuya wangka walytja kawalinanyi palu nganana nganampa wangka kanyini wantinytja wiyangku nganana tjukurpa wangkapai pakali puliringka munu inma kulu nyanpinytjaku nintilpai inma kalayaku inma wanampiku kulu kaya ngayula nguru nintiringkupai inmaku inkanytjikitja munu nyanpinytjikitja kulu.
The missionary been put church. Saturday, all the church coming up, and the people Christian. Christian leaders, everybody church leader now. We're interested in God's story. God, and my history underneath, both – kutjara.*	Wati mitjiniringku tjurtju tjunu ngura nyangangka ka anangu tjuta christinaringu munu kutjupa tjuta tjukurtjararingu ka kuwari anangu tjuta mukuringanyi tjukurtjara nyinanytjikitja Godaku warka palyantjikitja. Panya Godaku tjukurpa munu ngayuku ara kutjaratu tjungu ngaranyi.*

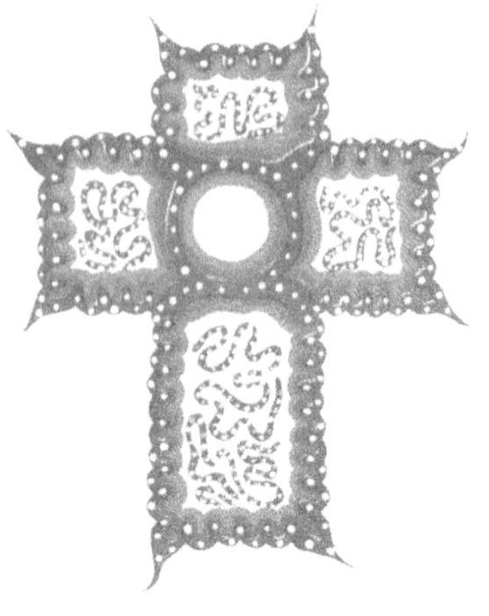

Design by Awulari Davey, from cover illustration of Ernabella choir cassette

* *Pitjantjatjara language proofreader, Bill Edwards, notes that the Pitjantjatjara translation does not mention 'underneath' (unngu in Pitjantjatjara), though it appears in the original English narration, which was visually enforced by gestures. It has been replaced in the Pitjantjatjara by a different spatialisation of the relationship of the two religious laws, reading 'God's word and my way both stand together'.*

4

the story of ernabella arts
tjukurpa ernabella artstjara

THE PAINTED STORY
TJUKURPA WALKATJURA TJAKULTJUNKUNYTJA

Makinti Minutjukur
(Translation by Ute Eickelkamp)

The painting and diagram on the following pages describe the Ernabella craftroom and how we have organised our work room over the years.

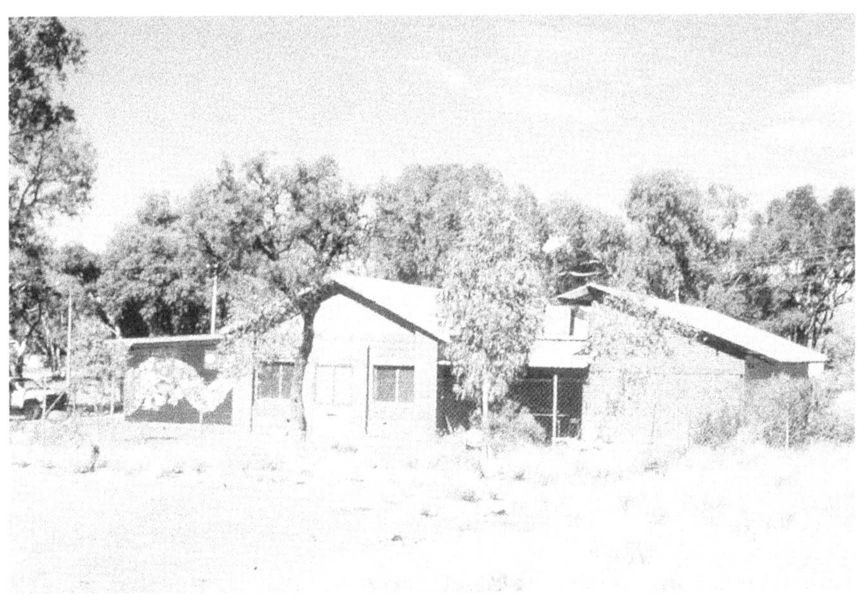

The craftroom at Ernabella, 1996 (photograph Ute Eickelkamp)

Section 1: Ngurangka
Nguranguru minyma tjuta ananyi warkaku craftroomakutu. Iriti craftrooma warka kutju ngarangi minyma uwankaraku.

Section 1: At home
From our camping grounds, the women used to go to work in the craftroom. In the past, this was practically the only employment opportunity for women.

Section 2: Craftroomangka
Craftroomangka, minyma pulka tjuta munu minyma tjukutjuku tjuta kungkawara tjuta uwankarangku warka kutjupa kutjupa palyalpai: Anapalaku walka floor rugangka palyalpai munu paperngka cardangka munu kuwari nguwanpa batikingka tjana palyani.

Section 2: In the craftroom
Women of all ages have been working together in the craftroom, doing different things, such as painting the Ernabella design on floor rugs and on paper cards and, more recently, in batik.

2a: Minyma kutjara-kutjarangku floor ruga kutjungka palyalpai.
2b: Ka kungkawara tjutangku cardpangka kutjungku kutjungku walka palyalpai.
2c: Batik palyantjikintjangku minyma tjutangku table walytja-walytjangka nyinara walka raikingka palyalpai mununya sharemilalpa waxpan.

2a: The women used to weave floor rugs, working in small groups on one piece.
2b: Younger women and teenage girls paint their designs on small cards, working separately.
2c: When creating batik textiles, the artists sit in family groups. Each woman uses her own little table to draw her design in wax onto the fabric. The waxpans are shared by the family group.

Section 3: Warkaku
Mission timeangka, minyma tjuta craftroomangka warkaripai palu mani tjukutjuku tjana mantjilpai. Munu tjinguru tjana ankupai kukaku maiku putikutu munu mantjilpai tjitjiku kuriku. Pirukuya tjana ankupai craftroomakutu karuwanu warkaku.

Section 3: About work
When Ernabella was a mission, many women worked in the craftroom, but they were paid only small wages. To supplement their provisions, they would go out bush and hunt game and collect vegetable food for their children and husbands. They would go back to work thereafter, crossing the creek on their way to the craftroom.

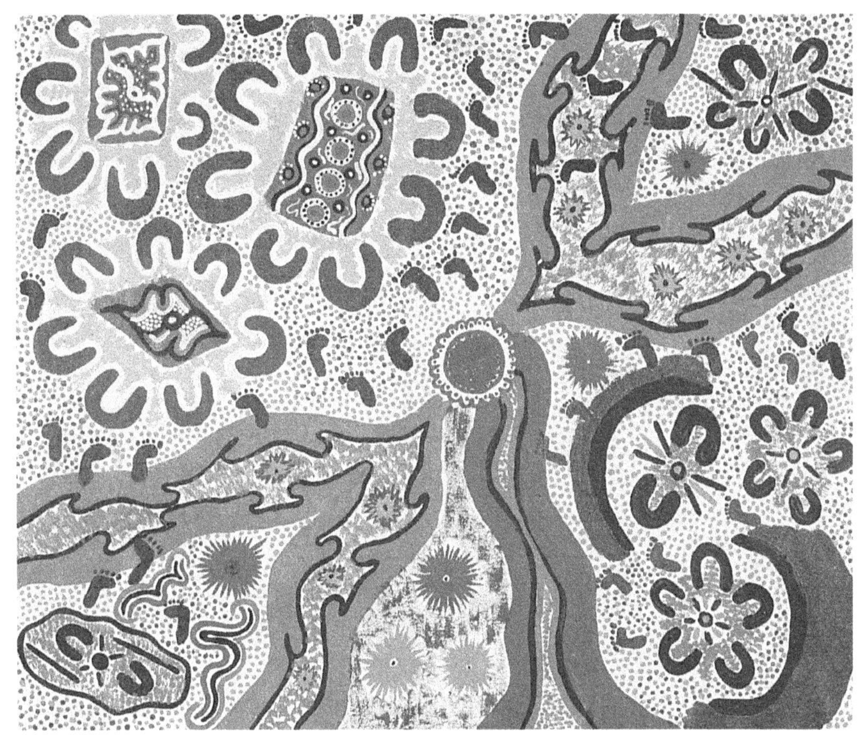

The craftroom story, by Makinti Minutjukur, 1996, gouache on canvas (Ernabella Arts collection, photograph Australian Institute of Aboriginal and Torres Strait Islander Studies)

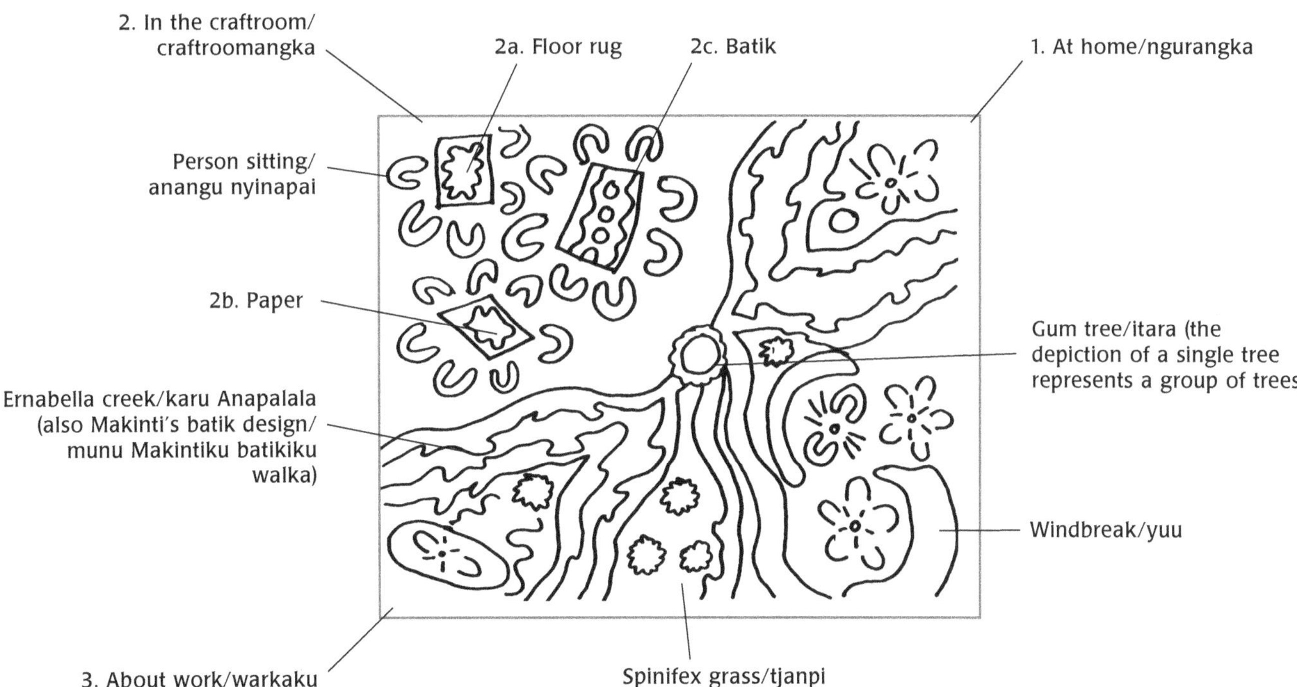

THE HISTORY OF THE CRAFTROOM
CRAFTROOMAKU TJUKURPA

(Translation by Kanytjupai Armstrong, compiled from several sources by Ute Eickelkamp)

1939

We started doing craftwork with Mrs MacDougall, making quilts, making baskets from spinifex grass* and knitting jumpers.

Craftwark startamilanu Mrs McDougallala munula mantara tjuta piti tjuta kulu kulu palyaningi tjanpi nguru munu ukiri nguru kulu munu tjampa tjuta kulu palyaningi.*

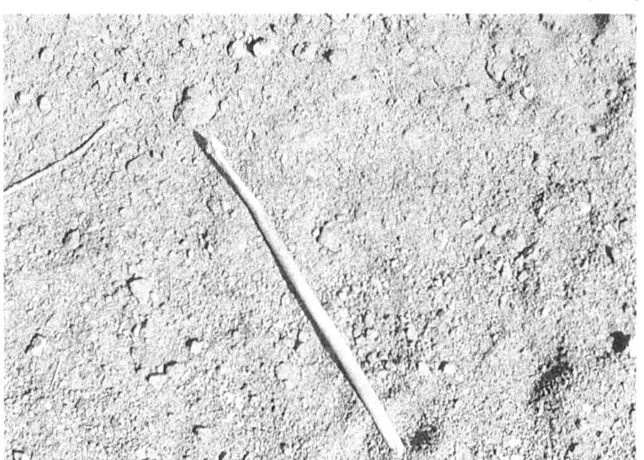

Crochet needle/pununguru nyiila purunypa palyalpai, carved by a woman in her seventies in 1996 (photograph Ute Eickelkamp)

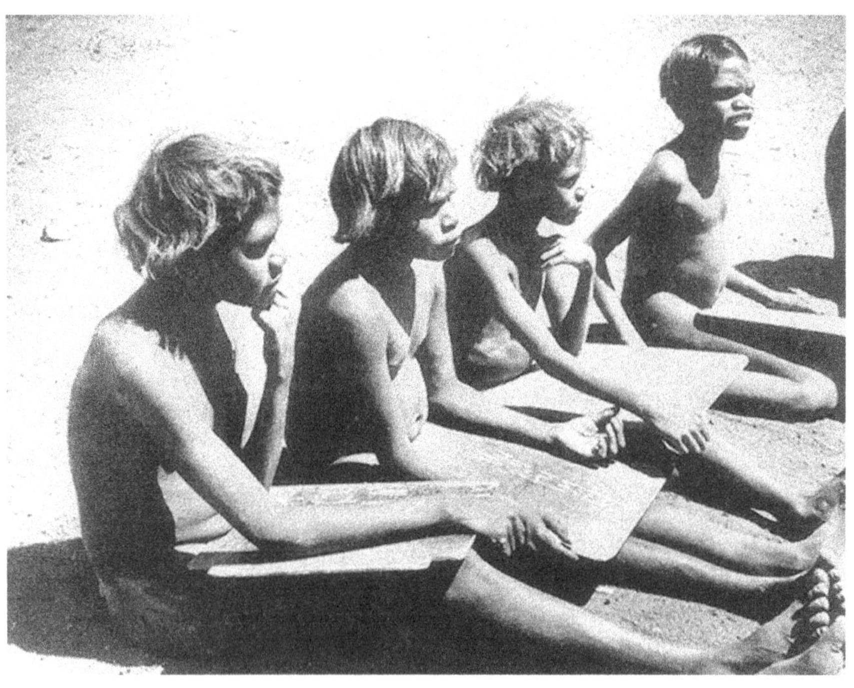

Open-air class, 1952 (girl to the very left, Dora Haggie, girl to the very right, Nellie Patterson) (photograph Reverend Hamilton Aikin #5341, source Presbyterian Church Trust Corporation, Victoria, courtesy Pitjantjatjara Council)

** Information by Mayawara Minutjukur; the rest of the text in this section is based on Mary Bennett's (personal communication) and Winifred Hilliard's accounts (articles in* Textile Forum *and personal communication) – the two previous art advisers – unless otherwise indicated.*

1940

When the school started in 1940, the children made drawings in Mr Trudinger's class.	Ka kuula tjunu kaya tjitji tjutangku arkara walkatjunangi Mr Trudingerlu nintilpai tjutangku.
Mr Trudinger gave them a little blackboard and they had white chalk.	Ka Mr Trudingerlu blackboard tjukutjuku tjananya ungu chalk piranpa kulu.

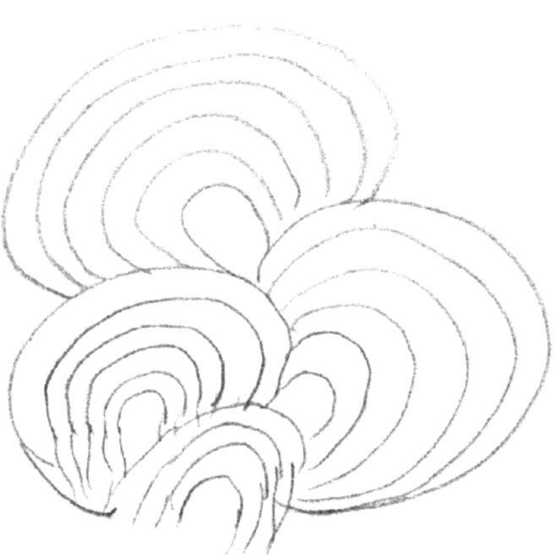

Langaliki's design from the early days of the craftroom, illustrated by Mayawara Minutjukur, pencil on paper, 1995. It is reminiscent of the women's and girls' woodcarving design, as Tjunkaya Tapaya, Mayawara's sister, has pointed out (Ute Eickelkamp collection).

Mayawara Minutjukur's very first design created at school on a blackboard, illustration by Mayawara Minutjukur, 1995 (Ute Eickelkamp collection)

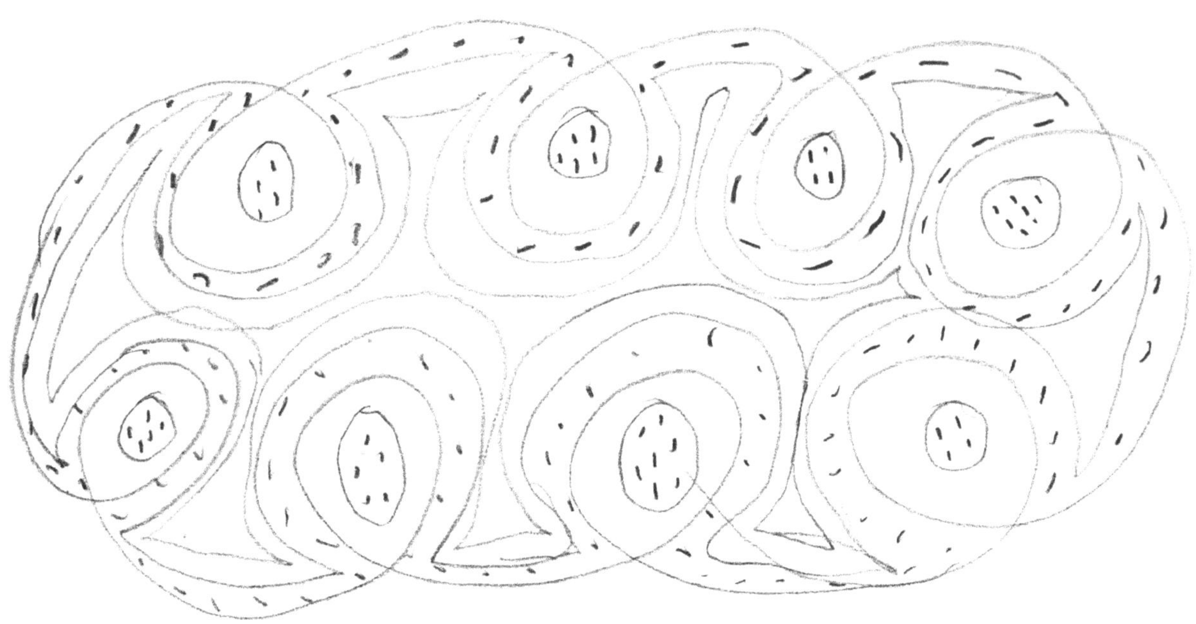

Ernabella schoolchildren with pastel drawings, 1958 (David Hewitt collection #399, photograph Nancy Sheppard, courtesy Pitjantjatjara Council)

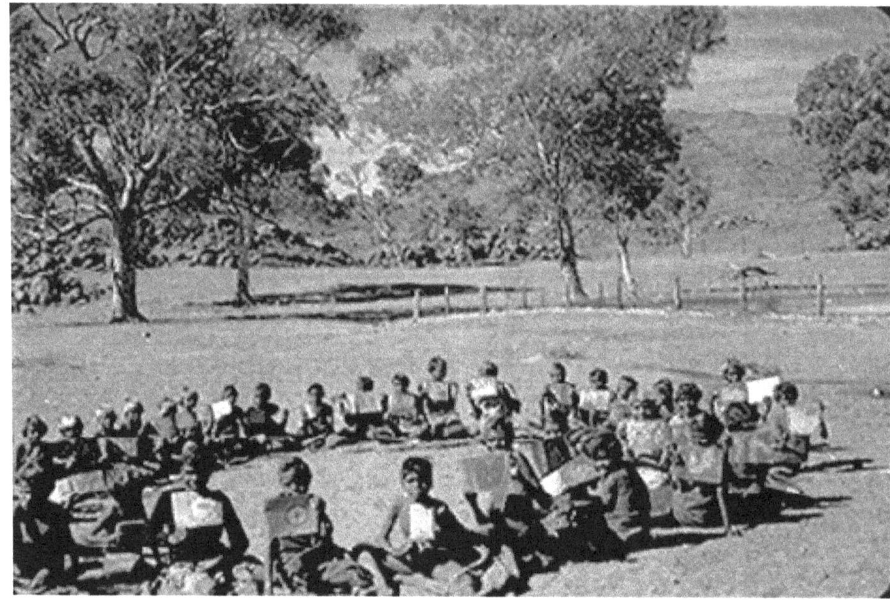

Ernabella school, 1955 (front left, Nungalka Stanley) (David Trudinger collection #4336, courtesy Pitjantjatjara Council)

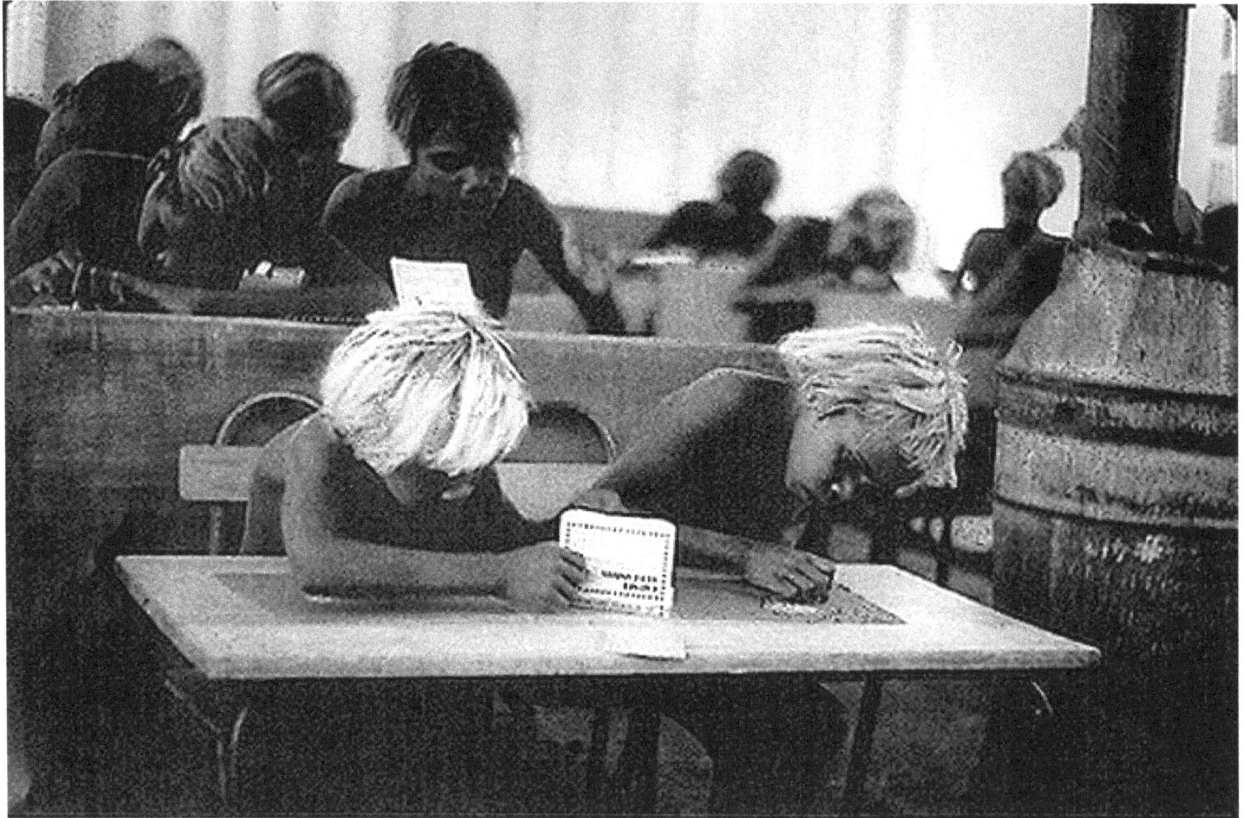

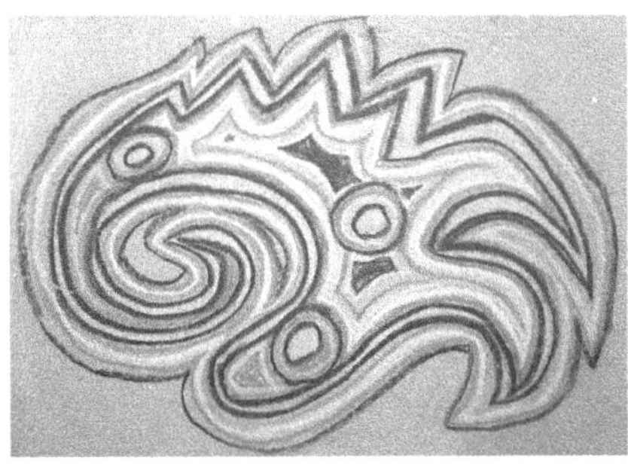

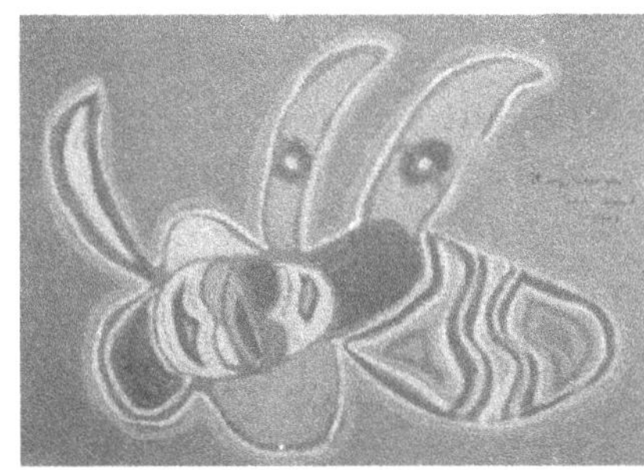

Far left: schoolchild's pastel drawing on cardboard paper, early 1950s (Winifred Hilliard collection, photograph Ute Eickelkamp)

Left: Nura Ward's pastel drawing on cardboard paper, 1952 (Winifred Hilliard collection, photograph Ute Eickelkamp)

We also made lots of drawings with colour pastels. In the old days, we only made the design on paper, at school. And from there, we went to the craftroom.

Kala walka kutjupa kutjupa kulu palyalpai crayonpangka. Iritila walka wiru tjuta palyalpai nyiringka kuulangka nyinara. Nyara palulangurula craftroomakutulta anu.

1948

In 1948, there was a terrible measles epidemic and everything stopped on the mission until it was over.

Nineteen forty-eightngka pika kura wirkanu ngananala ini panya measlepa ka kutjupa kutjupa tjuta ngara katingu pika paluru waintarinytjaku patara ngura nyanga Anapalala.

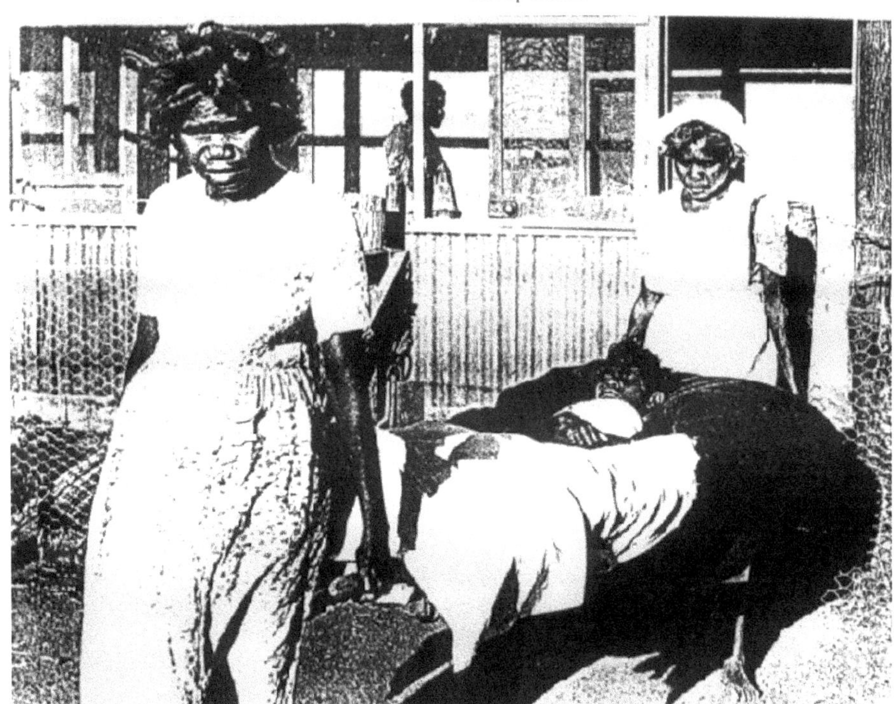

Ernabella clinic, late 1952 (Mayawara Minutjukur, right) (photograph Reverend Hamilton Aikin #5348, source Presbyterian Church Trust Corporation, Victoria, courtesy Pitjantjatjara Council)

Later that year, in December, Mrs Bennett from Kalgoorlie came to Ernabella. She advised us to spin hair and wool less tight. We've always known spinning, traditional way. Mrs Bennett taught us to weave on a small loom.

December 1948ngka malangka nguwanpa Mrs Bennettanya pitjangu Kalgoorlielanguru Anapalalakutu munulanya nintiningi mangka rungkantjaku woolpangka tjungura kala rawangku rungkara nintiringangi munulanya Mrs Bennettalu pulangkita loomangka palyantjaku nintinu loom tjukutjukungka.

Traditional spindle still used today (photograph Ute Eickelkamp)

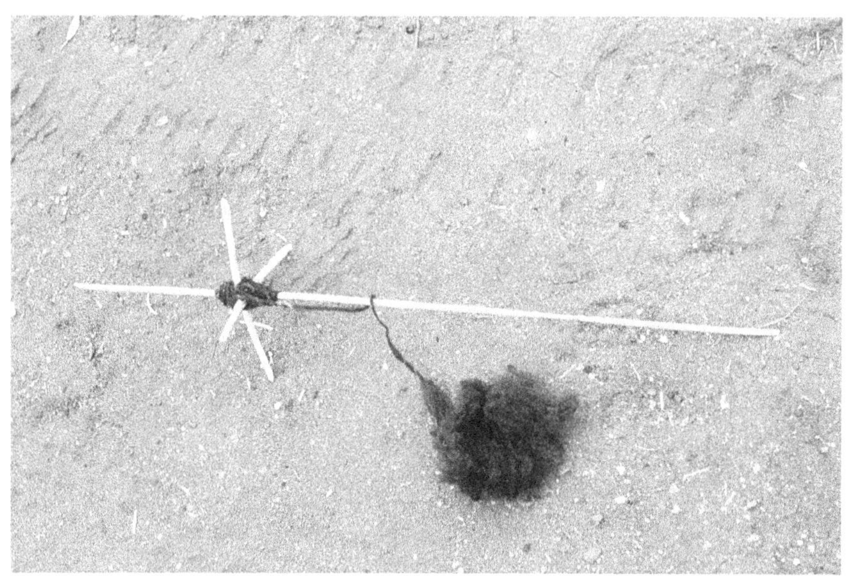

Nyukana Baker with one of her tapestries, probably early 1960s (detail) (Alice Peucker [Job] collection #4122, courtesy Pitjantjatjara Council)

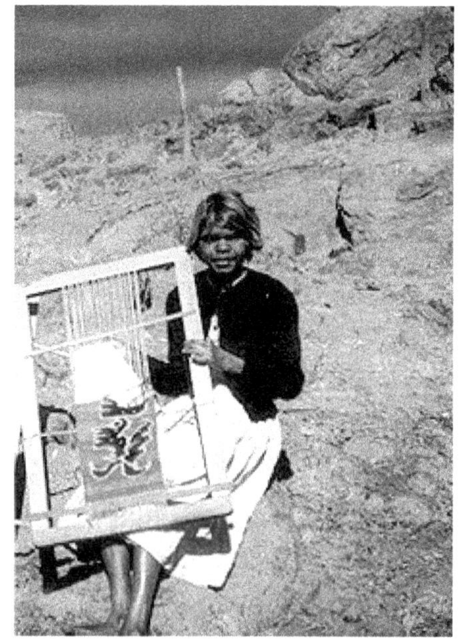

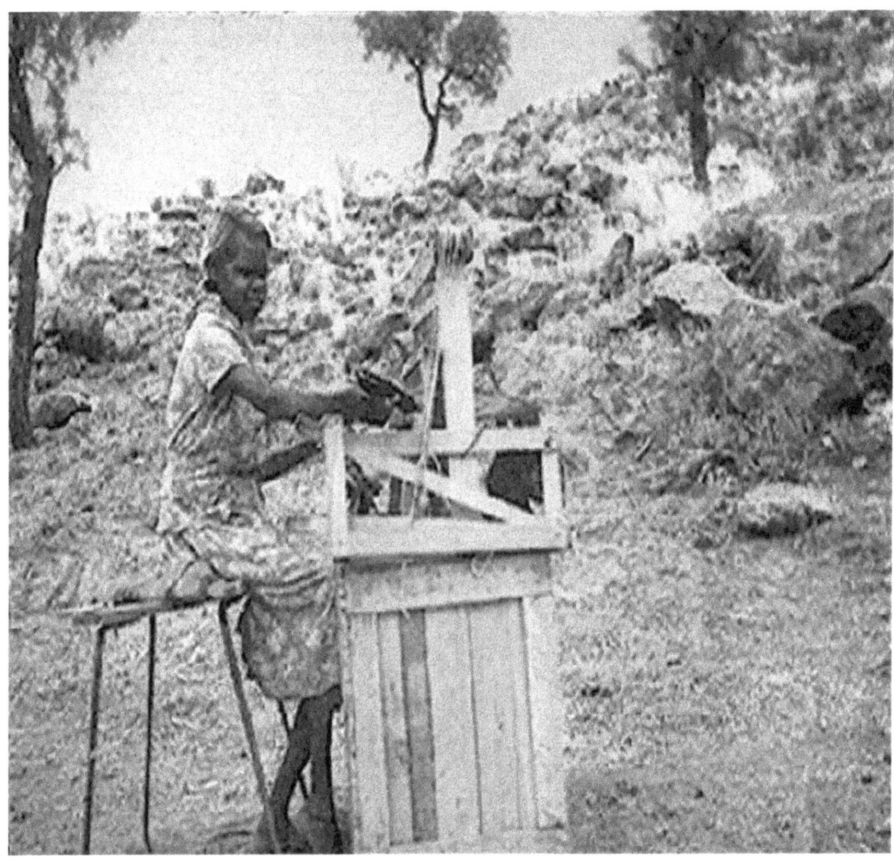

Left: Tjulkiwa from Amata on loom, Ernabella, 1954 (Ron Trudinger collection #4280, courtesy Pitjantjatjara Council)

Below left: schoolchild's pastel drawing, 1950 (Frank and Mary Bennett collection #3081, courtesy Pitjantjatjara Council)

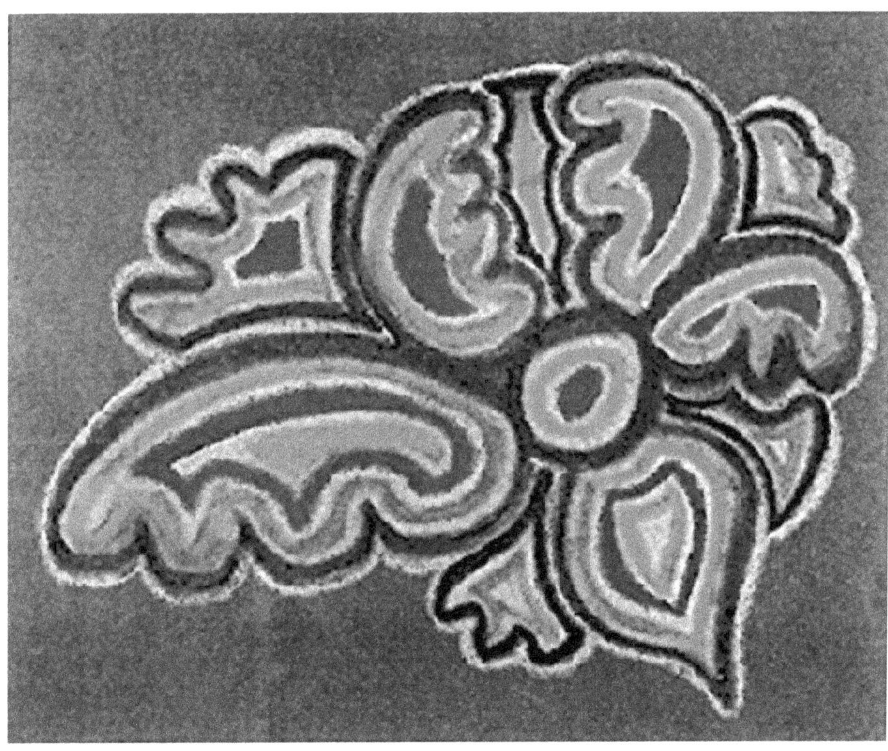

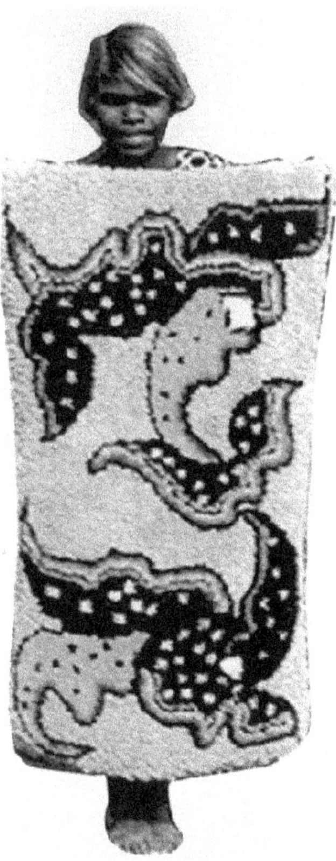

Nyukuna Baker with one of her hooked floor rugs, probably early 1960s (Alice Peucker [Job] collection #4013, courtesy Pitjantjatjara Council)

1949

Miss Baird (she became Mrs Bennett when she married) came from Adelaide and together with Mrs Trudinger we continued weaving.

We made hooked floor rugs decorated with the designs the schoolchildren had drawn. Some women made stitched patterns on hessian sugar bags. We also tried basketwork with plaited bought material.

This is how the craftroom began.

Munu 1949nta Miss Bairdanya Mrs Bennettanyaingu watingku altinyangka paluru Adelaidelanguru pitjala Mrs Trudingerla tjunguringu munula tjungungku mantara weavimilaningi.

Munula yakutja tjuta palyaningi palawa tjunkunytjaku ananguku walkatjara tjitji kuulitja tjutangku walkatjunkunytja tjara. Kaya minyma tjutangku wakara patiningi sugar tjunkunytjikitjangku yakutja tjuta munula piti kulu palyaningi mantarangka tjunngura wakara.

Nyanga alatji craftroom tjaataringu.

1950

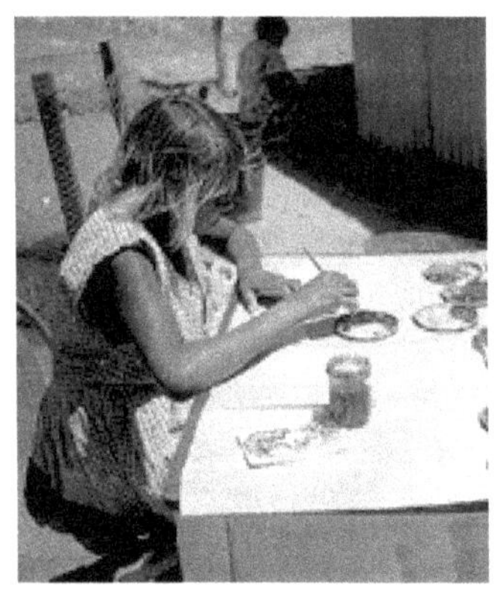

Angkuna Kulyuru, 1959 (John Fletcher collection #251, courtesy Pitjantjatjara Council)

The next year, around Christmas time, Miss Baird had the idea of asking the housegirls to paint greeting cards. The missionaries bought them all. The young artists still paint cards and bookmarks today.

Yiya kutjupa kulingka Miss Bairdalu kuliningi ngananala tjapintjikitjangku palumpa wali warka tjuta nyiri tjukutjukungka walka wiru palyantjaku nyiri nyara palunya tjananya panya mitjiniri tjutangku ngalyakatingu. Ka panyaya malatja tjutangku kuwari palyanitu nyiri tjutangka.

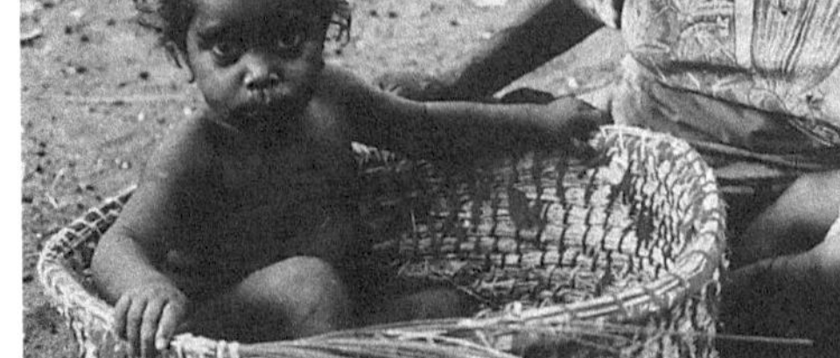

Pantjiti McKenzie with her nieces, 1995 (photograph Ute Eickelkamp)

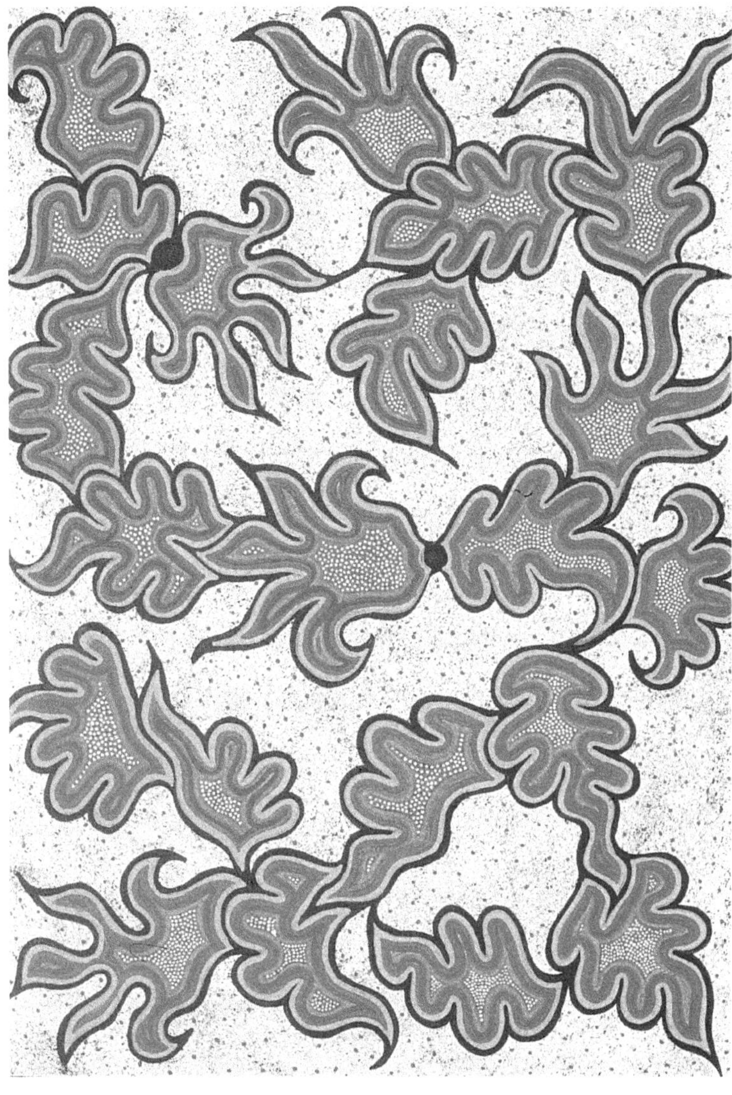

Recent acrylic painting on paper, by Tjunkaya Tapaya (Ernabella Arts collection, photograph Ute Eickelkamp)

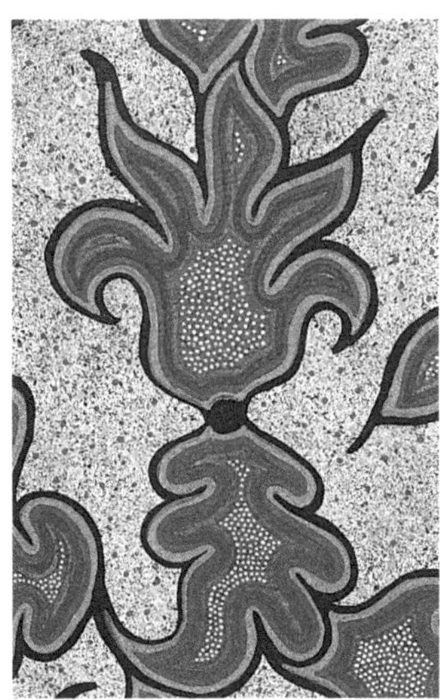

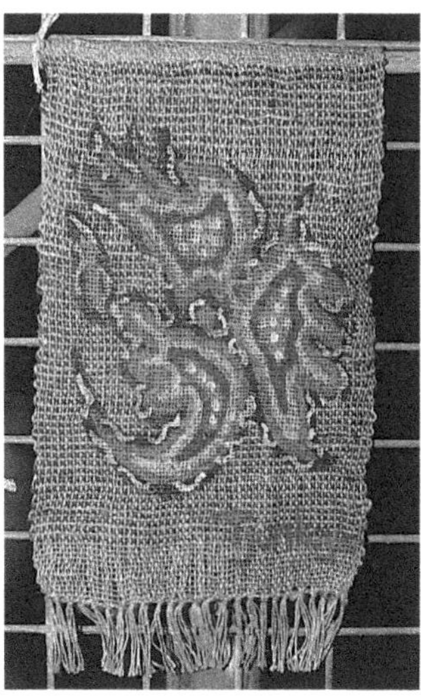

Far left: section of recent acrylic painting on paper, by Tjunkaya Tapaya (Ernabella Arts collection, photograph Ute Eickelkamp)

Left: small handwoven and painted wallhanging, by Tjunkaya Tapaya, 1950s (Ernabella Arts collection, photograph Ute Eickelkamp)

1952

Based on these early attempts to work with new techniques and materials, we went on designing canvas rugs and larger watercolours for sale.

Alatji palyaningi nganmanytju warka nyanga palunya tjananya munula nintiringangi warka kuwaritja tjutaku kulu mantara tjuta walkatjunkunytjikitja canvas tjuta rug wara tjukutjuku tjutaku kulu munu painta walka kutjupa kutjupa tjutaku kulu.

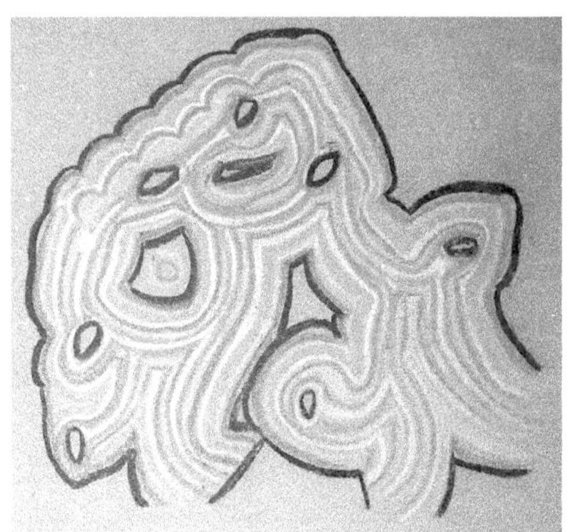

Pastel drawing, by Nyukana Baker, late 1950s (Winifred Hilliard collection, photograph Ute Eickelkamp)

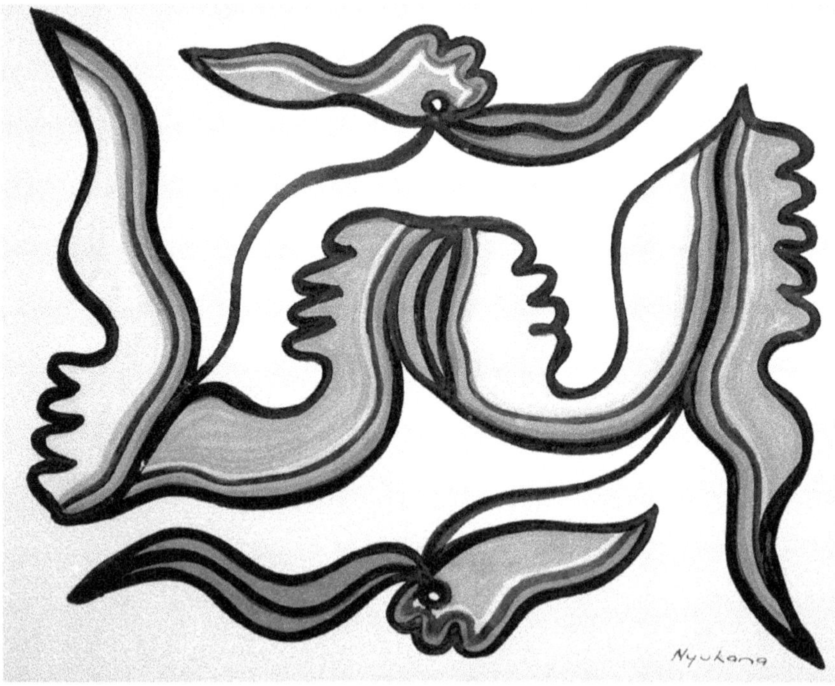

Watercolour on paper, by Nyukana Baker, late 1960s or early 1970s (Winifred Hilliard collection, photograph Ute Eickelkamp)

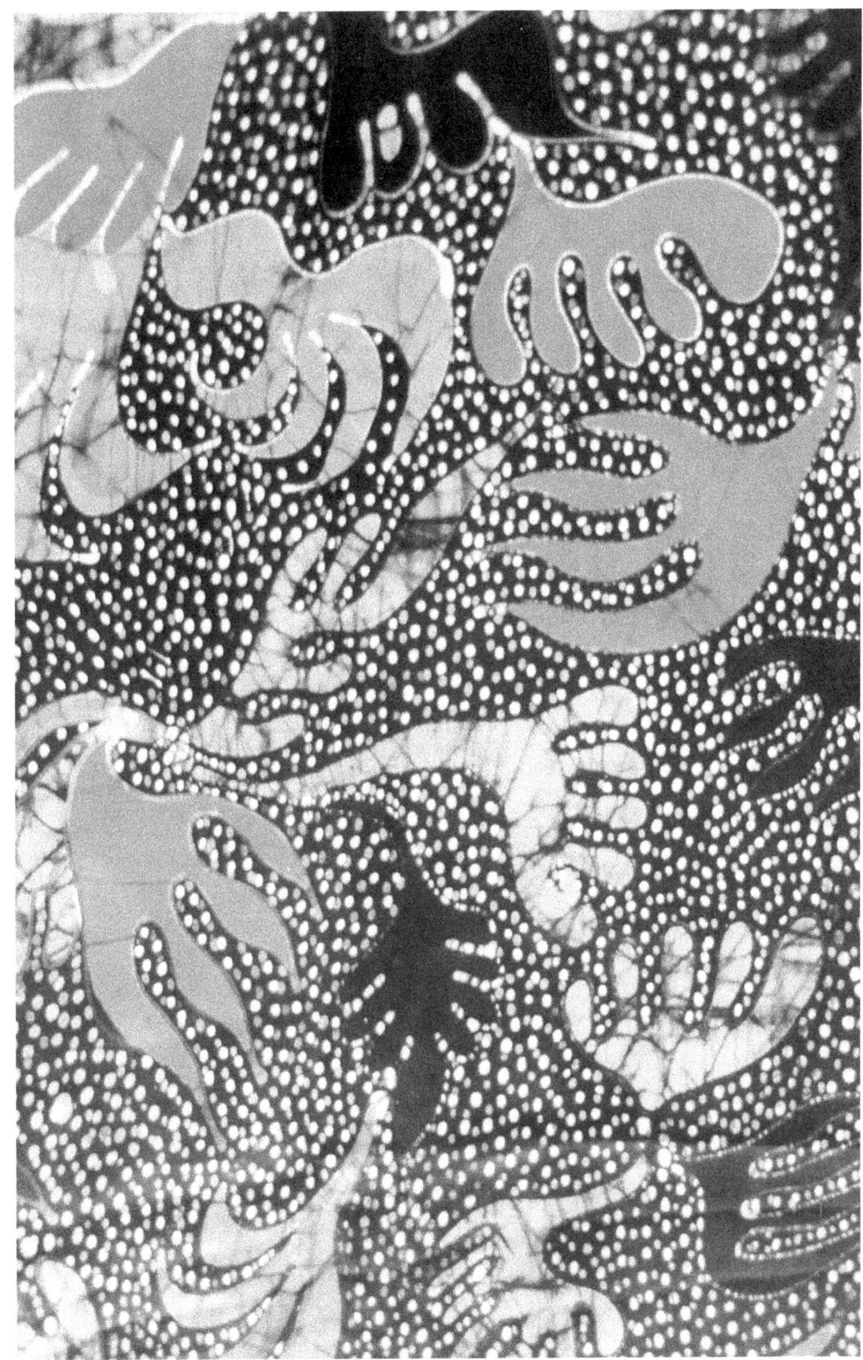

Silk batik (detail) by
Nyukana Baker, 1990s
(Ernabella Arts collection)

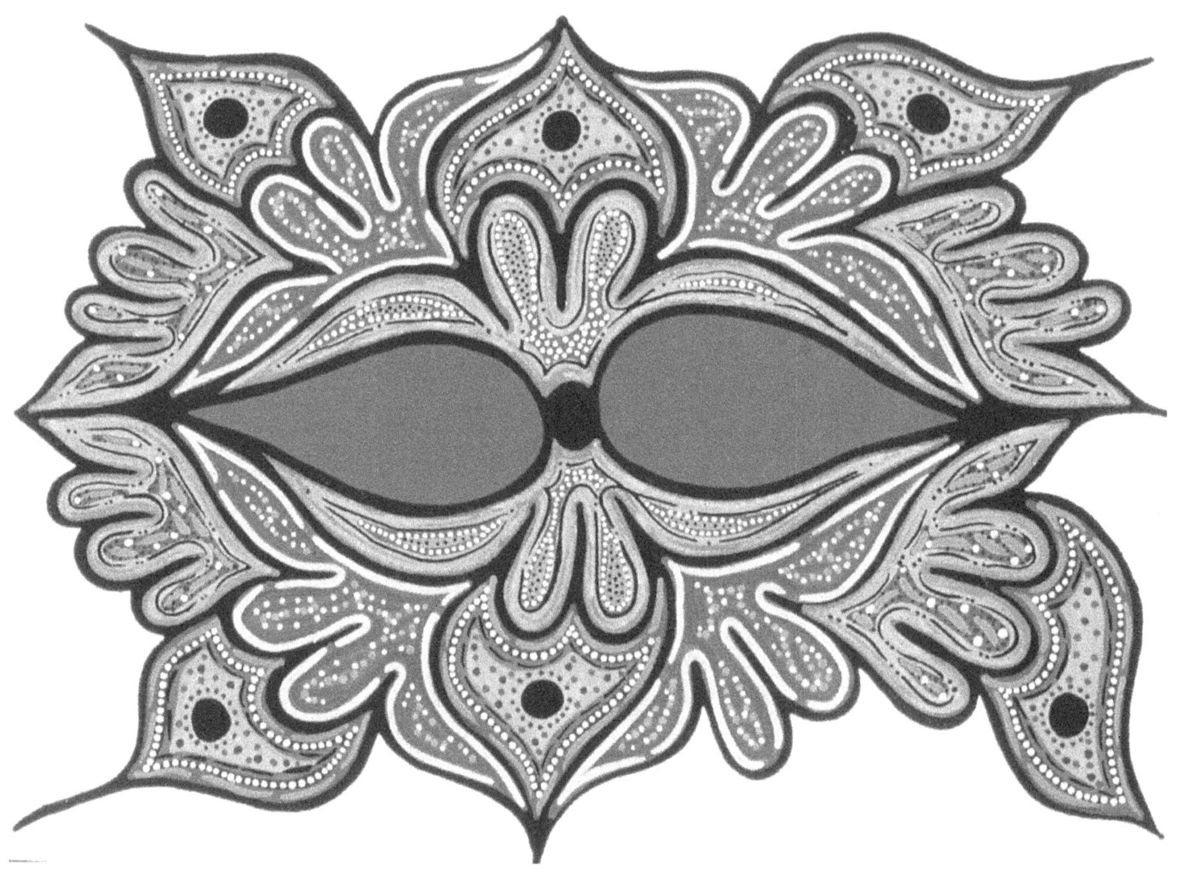

Acrylic painting on canvas, by Unurupa Kulyuru, 1990s (Ernabella Arts collection, photograph Ute Eickelkamp)

1954

Winifred Hilliard became our craft adviser. She stayed for 32 years and initiated marketing our art on a larger scale. With her, we made silk scarves with fabric paint, big murals, oil paintings on canvas and later in acrylic and gouache.

Winifred Hilliardanya nganampa craftroomaku mayatjaringu munu paluru nyinangi 32 yiya ngananala. Munulanya wiru tjutaku nintiningi kuwaritja tjuta walkatjunkula nintiringangi scarve tjuta painta minatjara oilatjara kulu canvasangka munu malangka acrylicatjara.

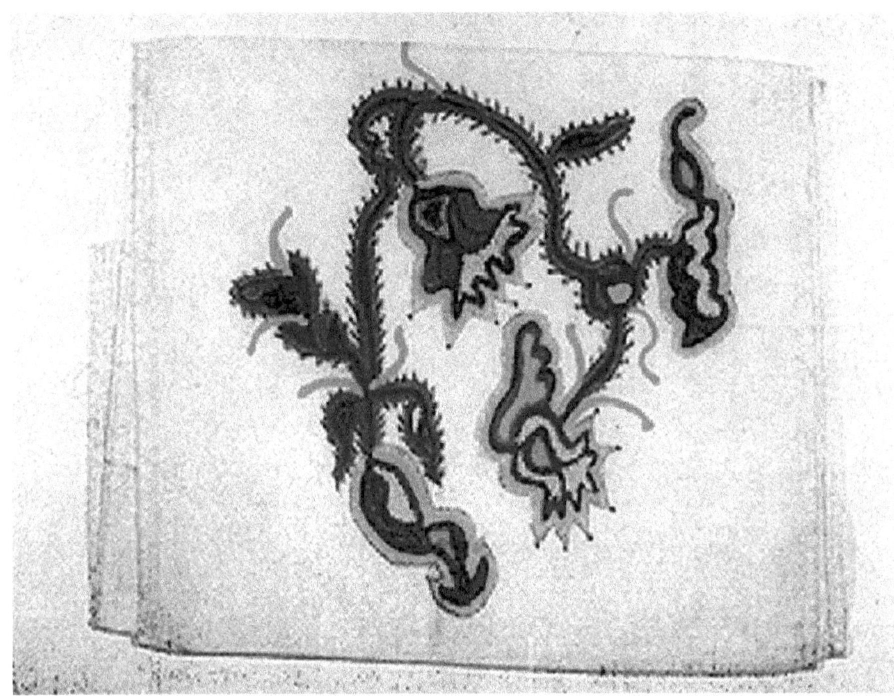

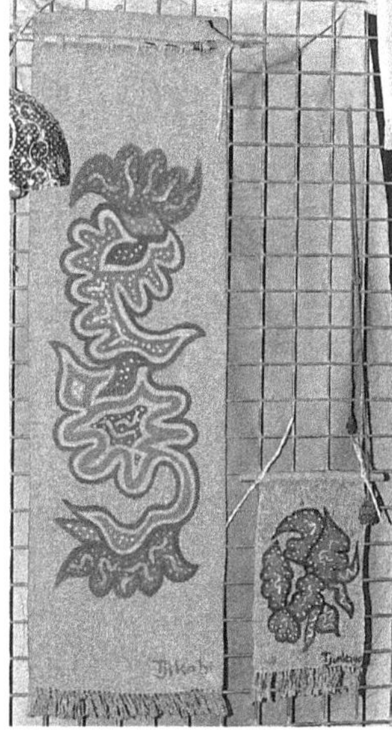

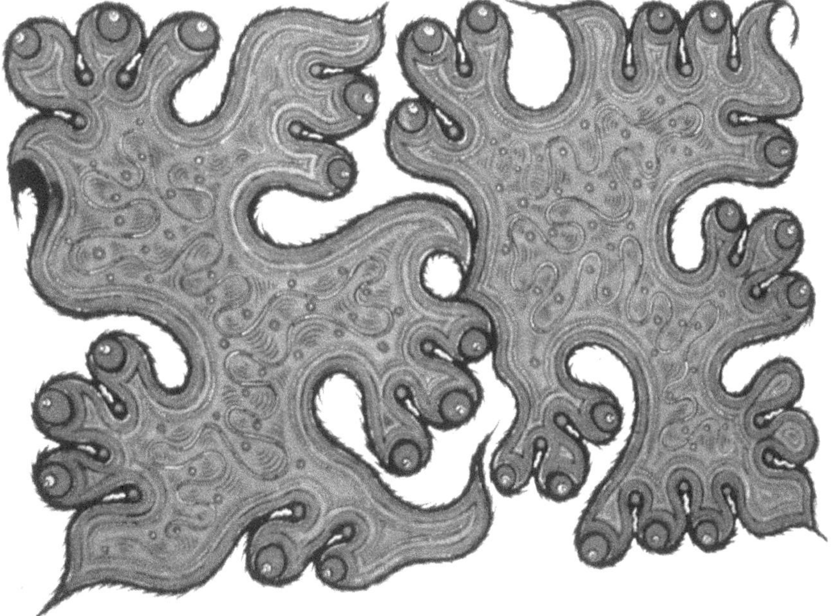

Above: wallhangings with painted designs by Tjikalyi Tjapiya (left) and Tjunkaya Tapaya (right), 1950s (Ernabella Arts collection, photograph Ute Eickelkamp)

Top left: handpainted silk scarf, artist deceased, 1960s (Frank and Mary Bennett collection #3068, courtesy Pitjantjatjara Council)

Bottom left: acrylic painting on board, by Makinti Minutjukur, late 1960s or early 1970s (Ernabella church collection, photograph Ute Eickelkamp)

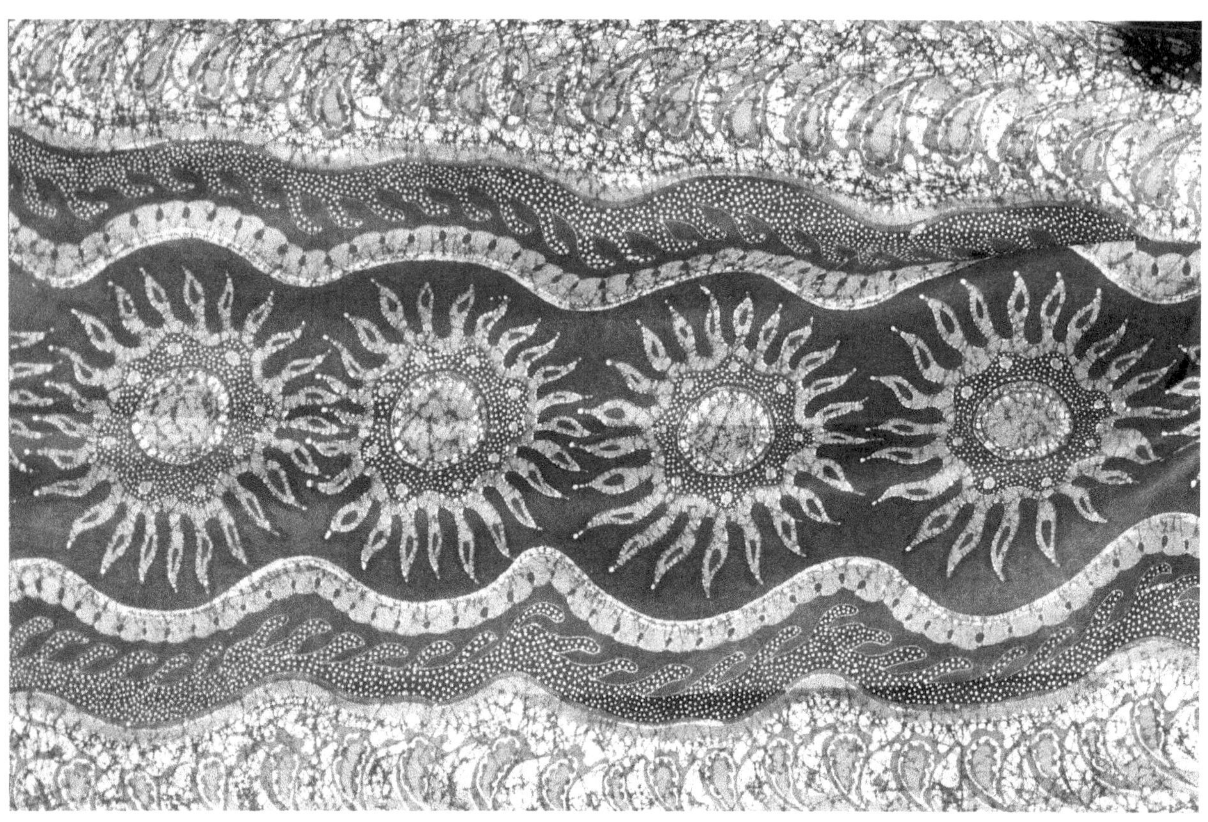

Silk batik, by Margaret Dagg, 1994 (photograph Ernabella Arts)

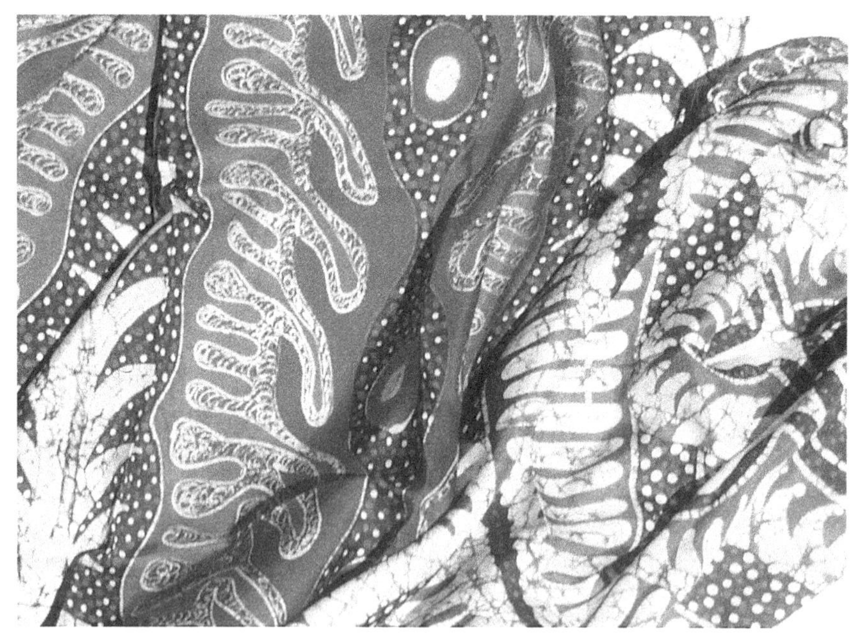

Silk batik scarves, by Inawintji Williamson (red) and Angkuna Kulyuru (blue), 1996 (Ernabella Arts collection, photograph Ute Eickelkamp)

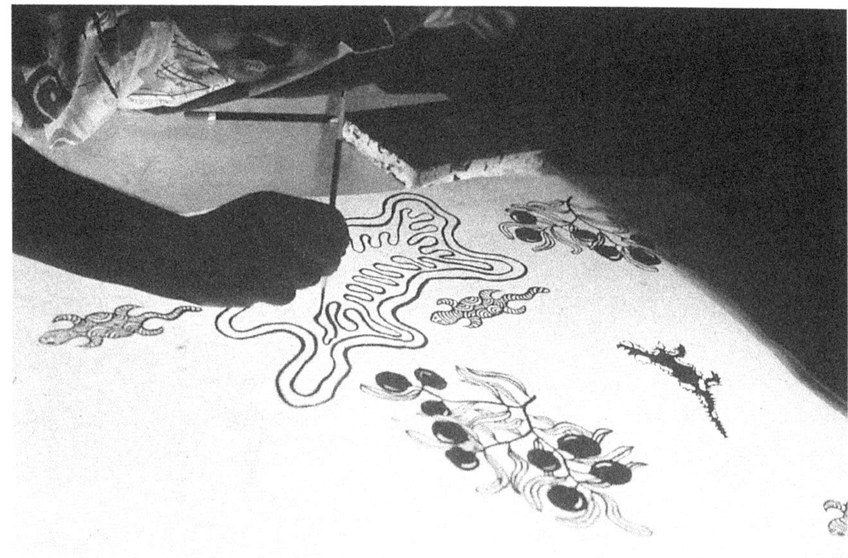

Nyuwara Tapaya creating a screenprint design, 1996 (photograph Ute Eickelkamp)

1972

The introduction of batik in 1972 had a great influence on our artistic development and the craftroom as a business. It's grown big since then.

Ka batik pakanu 1972angka kala wiru tjuta palyaningi paluru mukuringkunyangka ka warka nyanga paluru pakara pulkaringu munu kuwari ngaranyi.

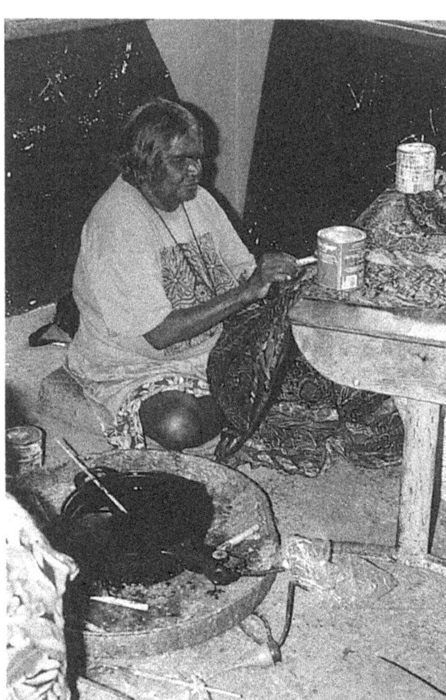

Senior artist Angkuna Kulyuru at her batik work place in the studio at Ernabella, 1996 (photograph Ute Eickelkamp)

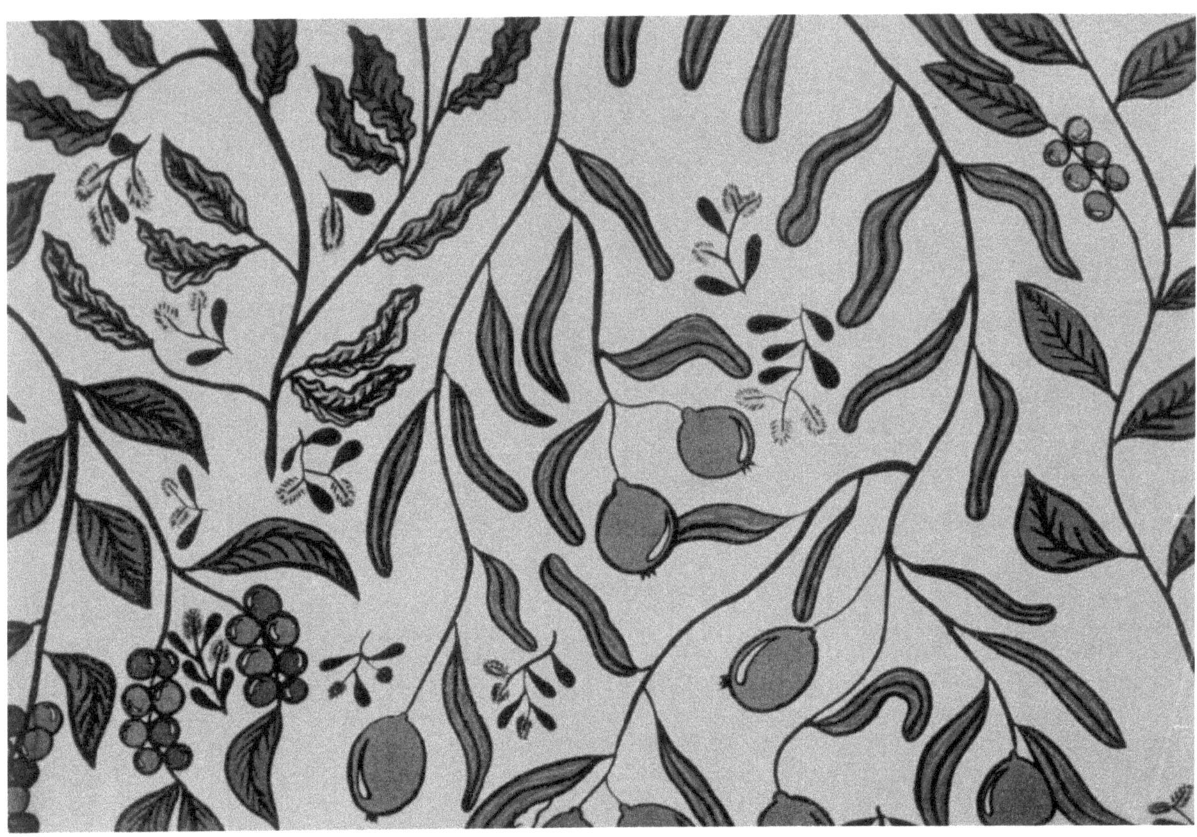

Bushfood/Mai putitja, by Nyuwara Tapaya, printer Marie Warren, screenprint on cotton fabric, early 1990s (photograph Ernabella Arts)

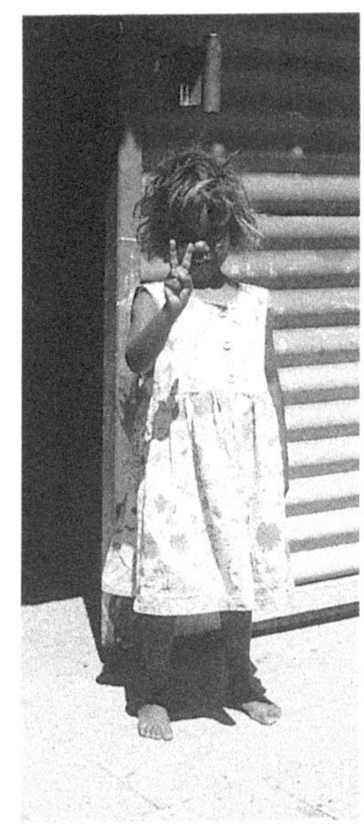

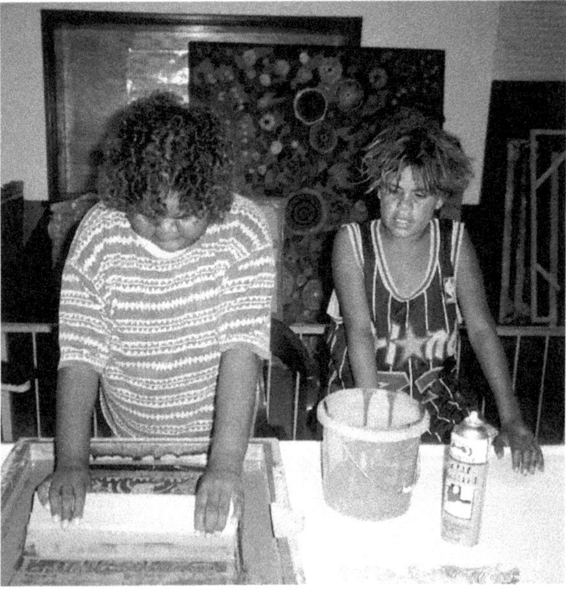

Right: Tanya Kunmanara wearing a dress produced with Ernabella Arts Trading, *Home/Nguratjara,* collective design, printer Marie Warren, screenprint on cotton fabric, late 1980s or early 1990s (photograph Ute Eickelkamp)

Far right: Nyuwara Tapaya (left) screenprinting, watched by Justin Wells, 1994–95 (photograph Ernabella Arts)

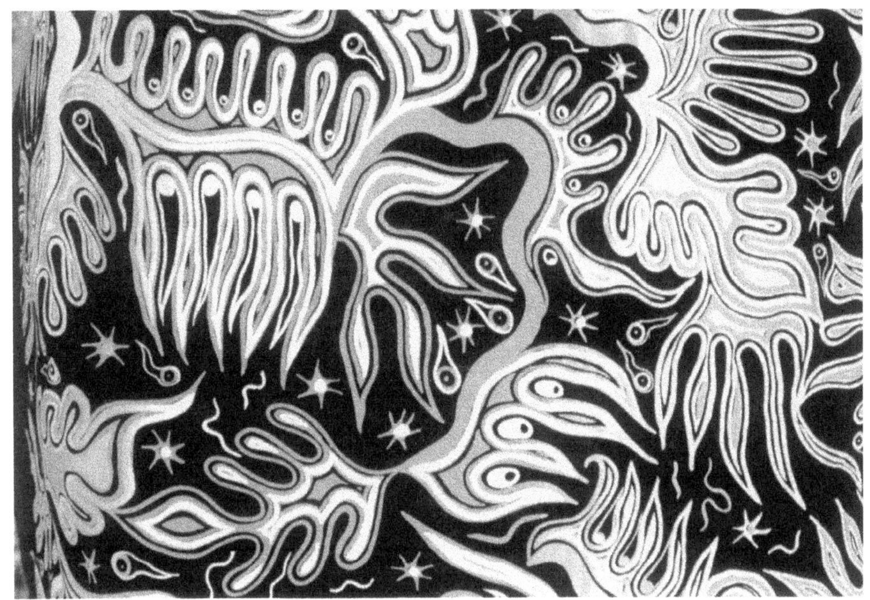

Bush/Puti, by Nyukana Baker and Nyuwara Tapaya, printer Marie Warren, screenprint on cotton, late 1980s or early 1990s (photograph Ernabella Arts)

Silk painting (detail), by Awulari R (Rita) Davey, 1996 (Ernabella Arts collection, photograph Ute Eickelkamp)

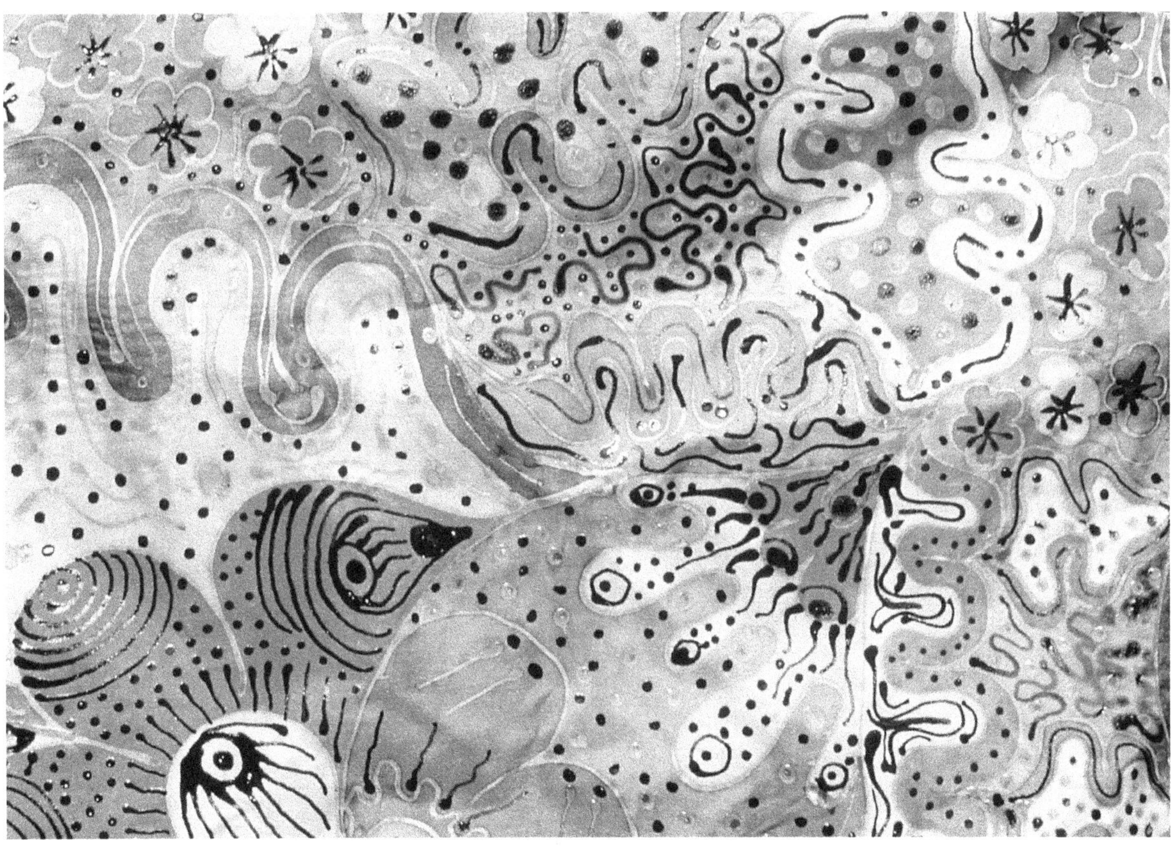

Silk painting (detail), by Alison Carroll, 1995 (Ernabella Arts collection, photograph Ute Eickelkamp)

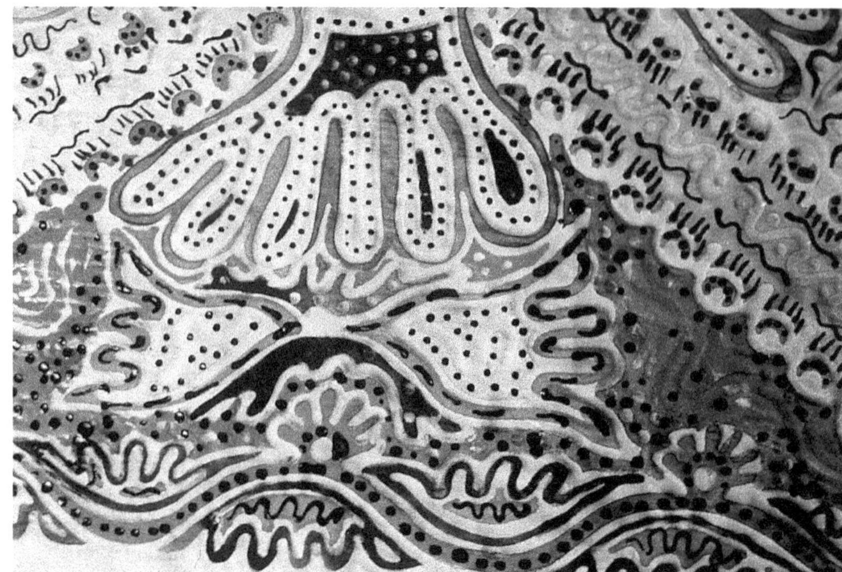

Fire/Waru (detail), by Nyuwara Tapaya, 1993, lithographic offset print on paper (Ernabella Arts collection, photograph Ute Eickelkamp)

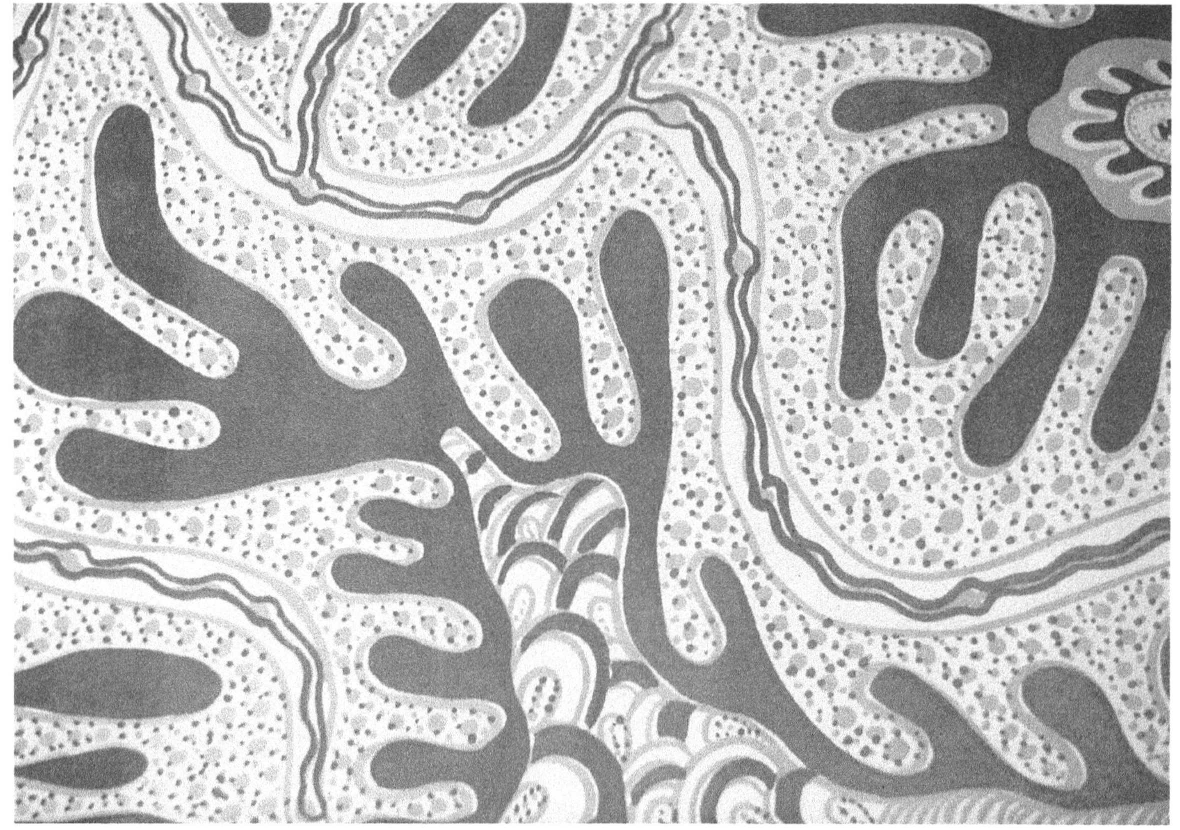

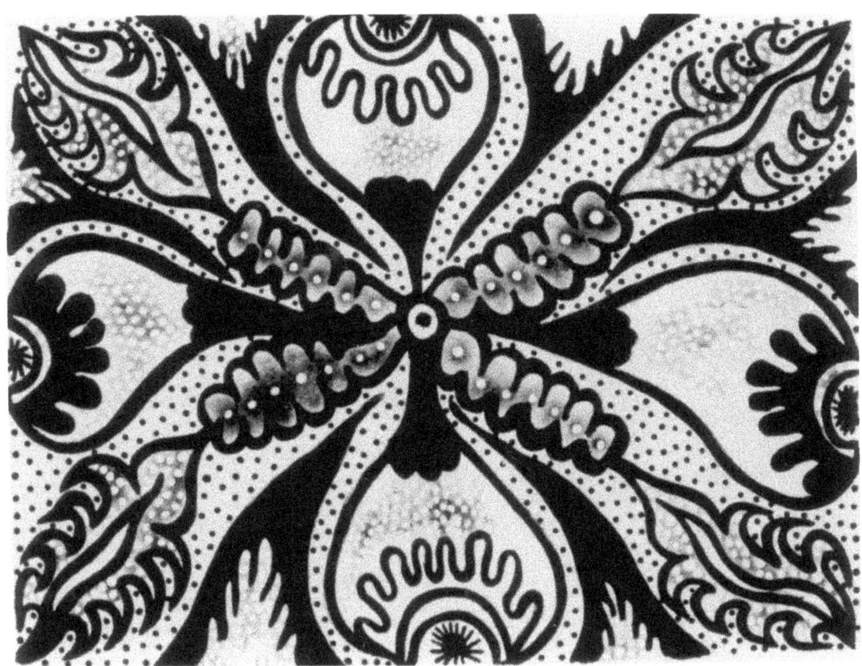

My best design/Ngayuku walka wirunya, by Angkuna Kulyuru, 1990s, lithographic offset print on paper (Ernabella Arts collection)

We are constantly learning new techniques, exploring our skills in different media, like etching, screenprinting, silk painting and, most recently, solarplate printmaking – all with our design.

Kala pulkara nintiringanyi munula walka kutjupa kutjupa palyani raikingka nyiringka kulu kulu ananguku walka.

There are two other important artworks we produce: one is woodcarving, which is based on traditional skills and done by both men and women out at the campfires. Most punu are marketed through Maruku Arts and Crafts.

A few years ago, we started telling stories about life in a community and our problems, and also about traditional law. Those stories are told on canvas using the iconography from other Western Desert people (Pintupi, Aranda, Luritja).** In this way, Aboriginal people can understand them across language boundaries.

Ka warka pulka kutjara kutjupa panya punu palyantja minymaku watiku kulu warka nyanga paluru warka nyanga palunyaya ngura walytjangka palyalpai munu walkatjura ungkupai Maruku Art Craft.

Kala kuwari nguwanpa panya yiya nyaranta tjukurpa tjuta tjakultjunangi nganampa wankatjara nganampa nguraku kutjupa kutjupa tjuta pakantja ngananala ka tjukurpa paluru tjana canvasngka ngaranyi wangka kutjupangku kutjupangku palyantja anangu Pintupingku Arandangku Luritjangku nyanga alatji nyakulaya anangu tjutangku kulira nintiringkuku.**

*** Although Arrernte is now the accepted spelling, the Pitjantjatjara use Aranda and so this spelling has been retained here.*

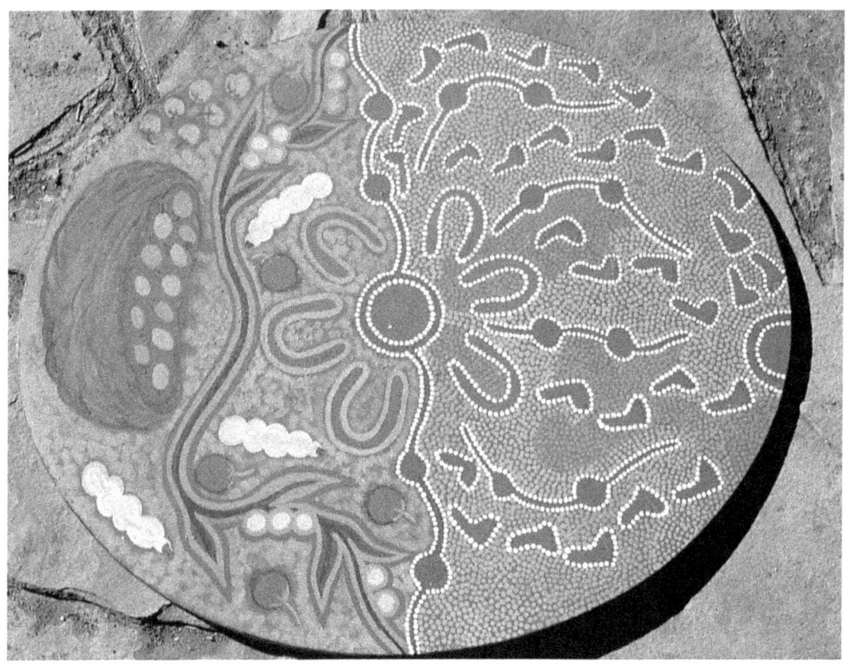

Acrylic painting on canvas, by Audrey Brumby, 1990s (Ernabella Arts collection, photograph Ute Eickelkamp)

TJULKIWA'S FATHER'S STORY OF ARALYA
TJULKIWAKU MAMAKU TJUKURPA ARALYANYATJARA

(Translation by Kanytjupai Armstrong)

Young women were making camp at Aralya when heavy rain and hail came down. One young fellow had fallen asleep and the girls kept trying to wake him up. But he wouldn't, he was fast asleep. So he was killed by the hail falling down on him. The young women sought shelter in a large cave, 'Kuridi', and they were safe.

Kungkawara tjutangku ngura palyanu Aralyanya ka mina pulka kunatatjara pitjangu munu tjananya pulkara puyiningi ka nyiinka kutju nyara palula kunkunpa pulka ngaringi kaya kungka panya tjutangku putu wankaningi ka paluru kunkunpa alatjitu ngaringi ka kunatangku kunkunpa alatjitu atura iluntanu kaya kungka panya tjuta kutju kulpi pulkangka tjarpara wankaringu.

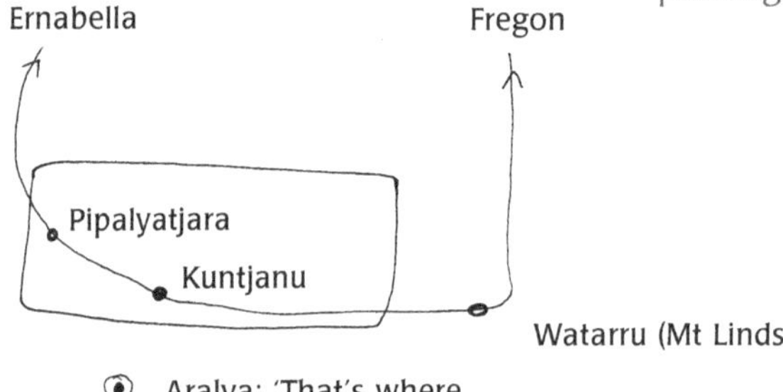

Area of Tjulkiwa's father's story about Aralya (sketch reproduced by Ute Eickelkamp from the artist's sand drawing)

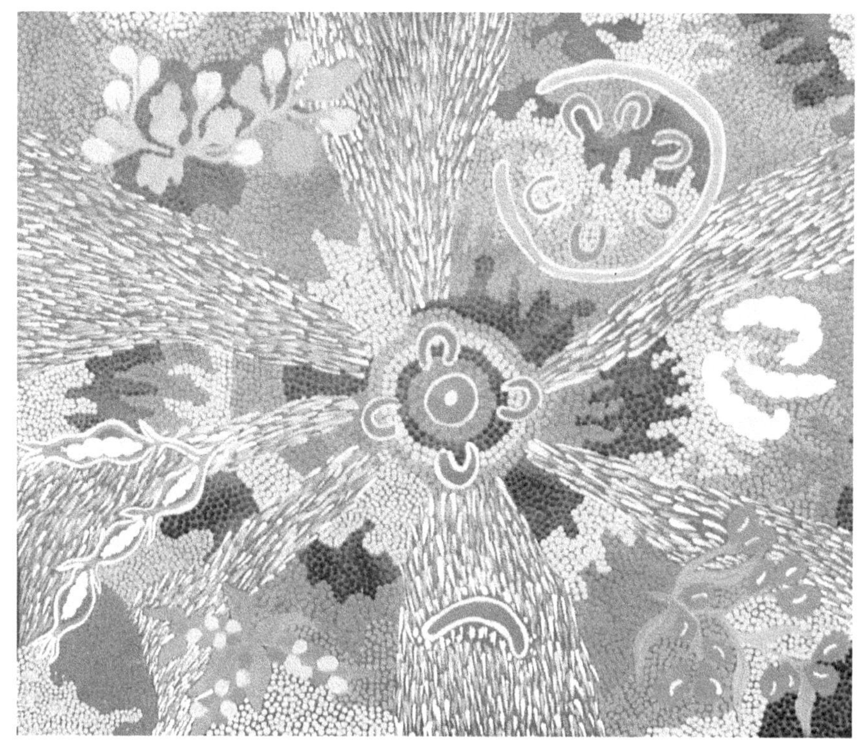

Aralya, by
Tjulkiwa Kunmanara, 1990s,
acrylic painting on canvas
(Ernabella Arts collection,
photograph Ute Eickelkamp)

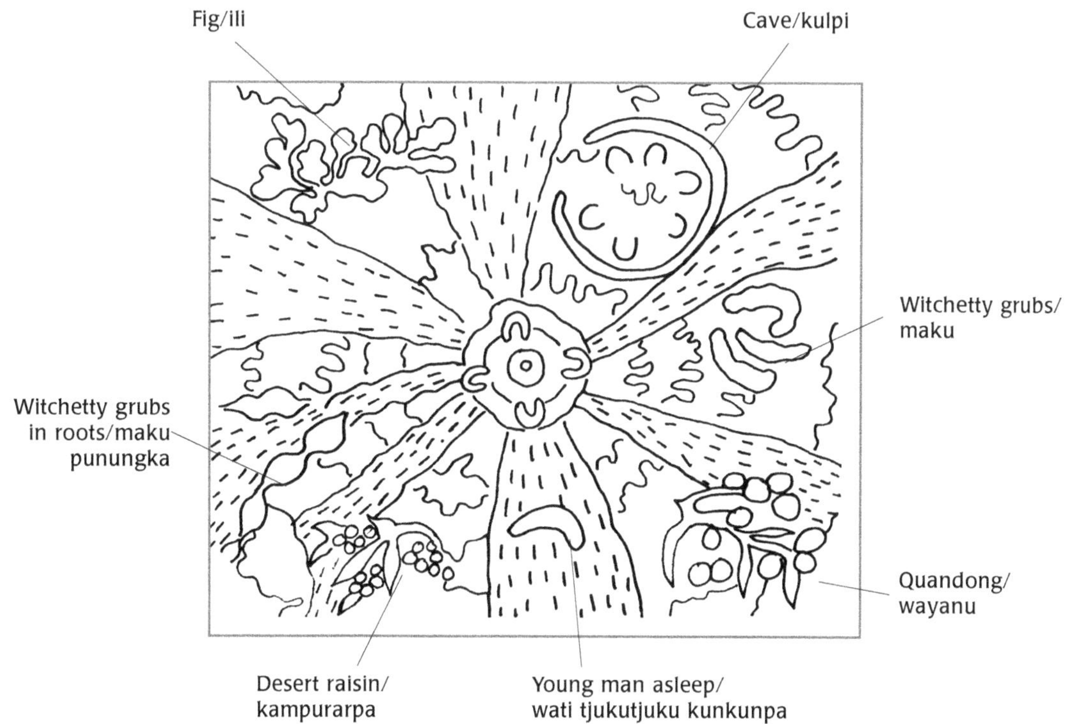

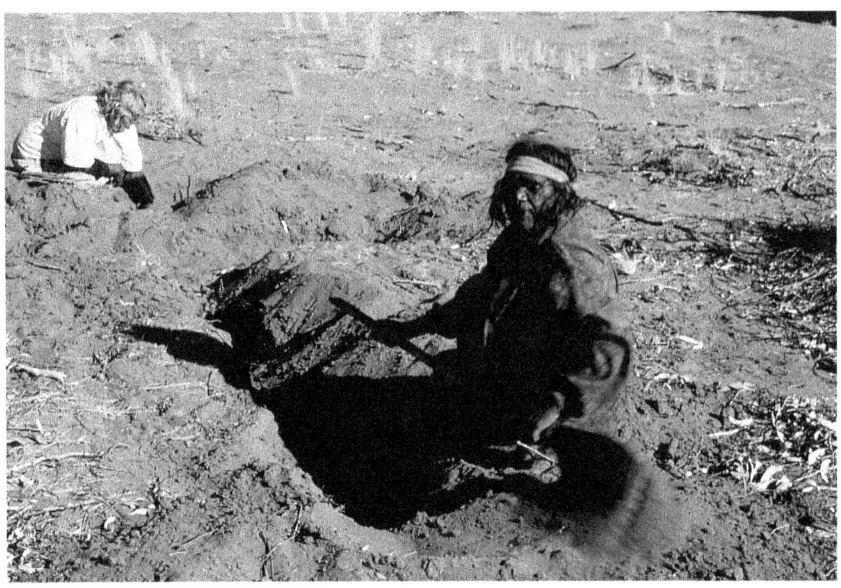

Kunmanara Jacob (background) and Pantjiti McKenzie digging up roots of eucalyptus trees for woodcarving, 1996 (photograph Ute Eickelkamp)

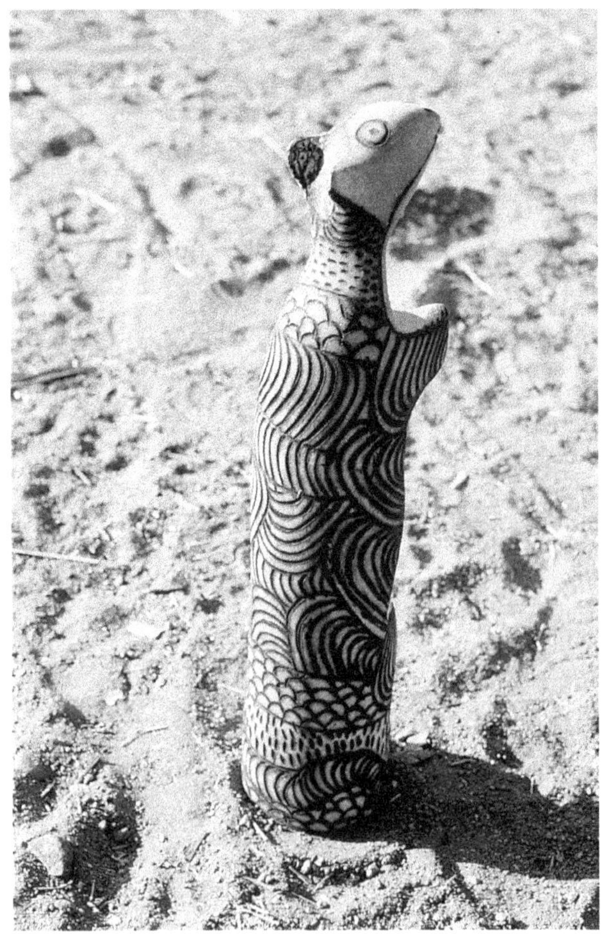

Rabbit sculpture, by Nura Rupert, 1996 (photograph Ute Eickelkamp)

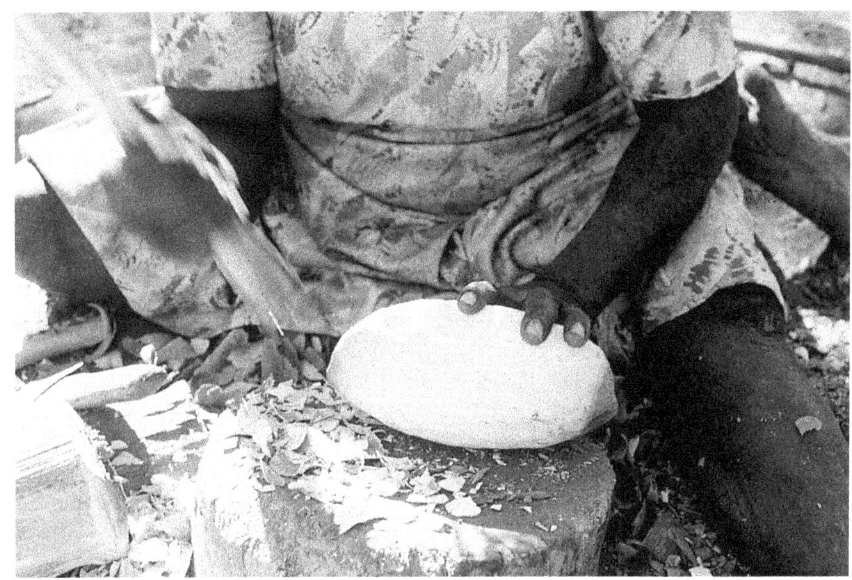

Pantjiti McKenzie carving a small carrying dish, 1996 (photograph Ute Eickelkamp)

Yangkuyi Yakiti applying pokerwork design on music sticks, 1996 (photograph Ute Eickelkamp)

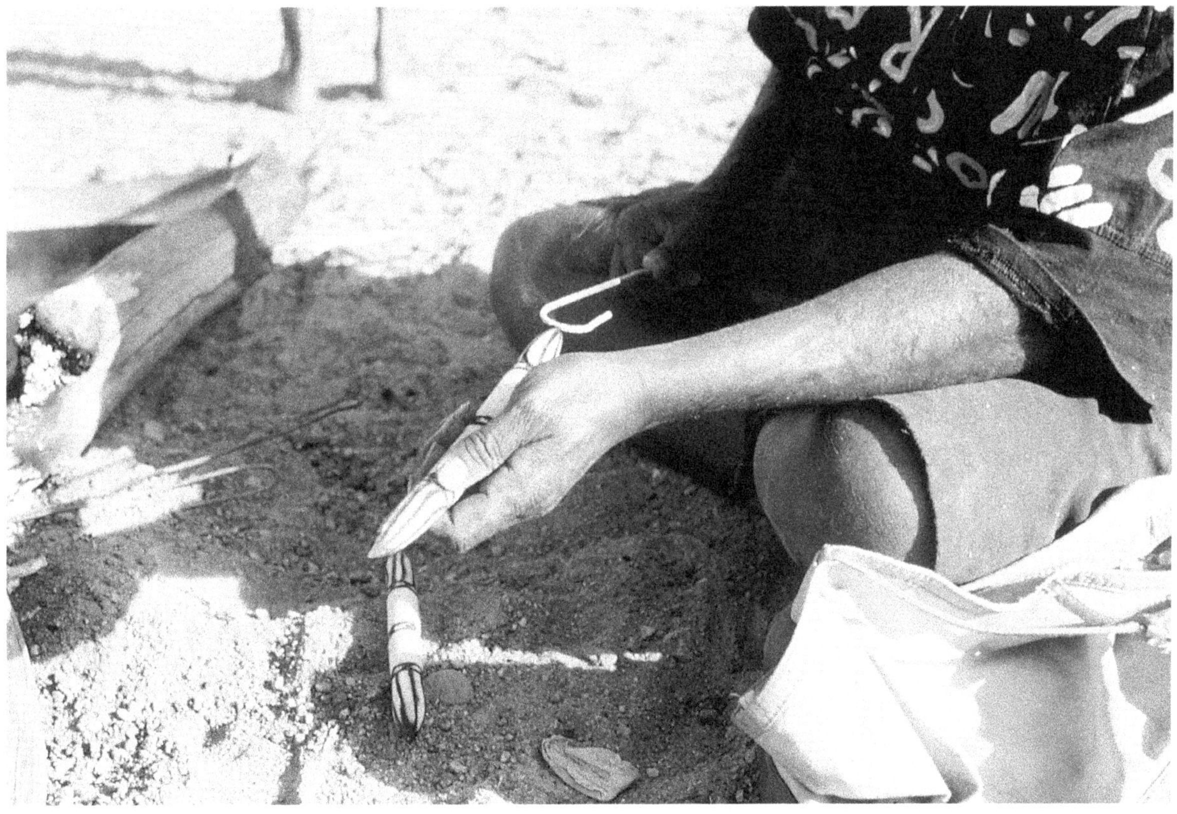

OUR DESIGN
NGANAMPA WALKA

Alison Curley and Kunmanara Brumby

We didn't draw the Ernabella design in the sand before white man came, but animal tracks and milpatjunanyi.

Nganana nganmanytju Anapalaku panya walka walkatjunkunytja wiyatu mantangka wati piranpa pitjanytja kuwaripangka palu kuka tjina tjuta kutjula walkatjunkupai munula milpatjura mantangka walkatjunkupai.

Tjikalyi Tjapiya

We're not telling stories. When Nyukana finishes a painting, she can't tell a story. I can't too. We don't think too long, pick it up [the pencil] and when it's finished, the woman thinks, 'I leave it like that, it's pretty'.

Don't ask for stories. This is not a sacred one, wildflower wiya. It comes from our mind and from our heart.

Nganana Nyukanaku walkaku ngurpa putula tjakultjunanyi ka paluru tjukurpa walkatjunkunytjatjanungku pututu tjakultjunanyi ngananala patu rawangku kulintja wiyangku pintjila mantjira walkatjura. Ka wiyaringkunyangka minyma tjutangku kulilpai kana alatji alatjitu wanti wiru mulapa nyangatja ngarangi.

Piruku tjukurpaku tjapintja wiyangku wantima nyangatja tjukurpa milmilpa wiya nyangatjala. Nganana kulira walkatjunkunytja.

We make lines, follow this direction, then I look and go the other way. Wiru, beautiful.

Munula laini palyaningi tjukarurungku kana ngayulu kampa kutjupa nyangu wiru mulapa.

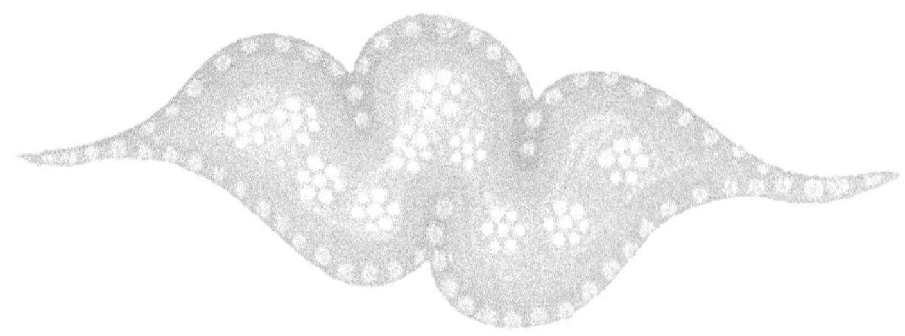

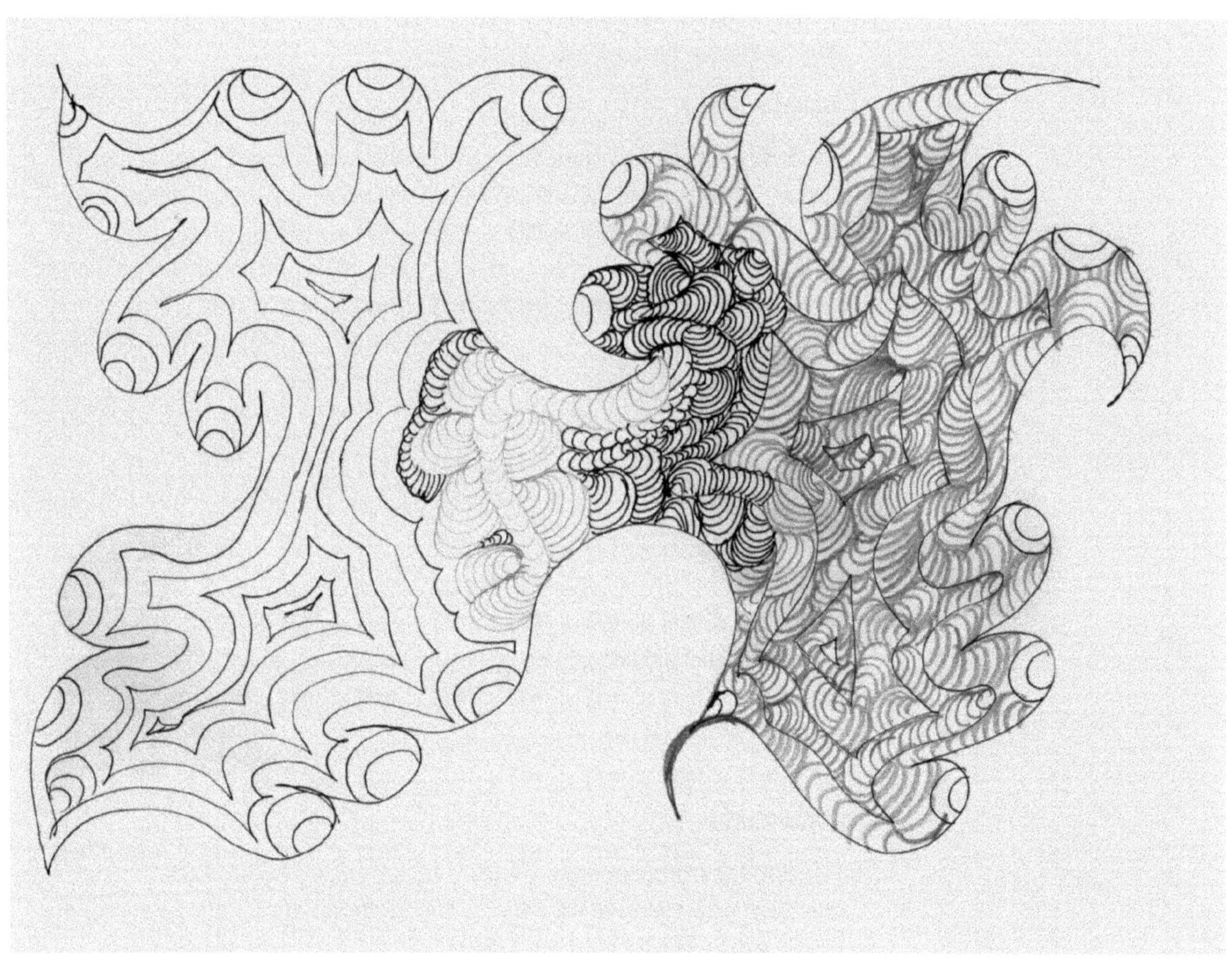

Design illustration by Tjikalyi Tjapiya, pencil on paper, 1995: the left part of the design shows the design style in drawings and paintings, and the right part illustrates the woodcarving decorative design style, with the latter demonstrating the change of directions during the process of composition (Ute Eickelkamp collection).

LEARNING THE DESIGN
NINTIRINGANYI WALKAKU

(All translations by Kanytjupai Armstrong, except Lucy Lester's, as she provided a translation of her own text into Yankunytjatjara.)

Margaret Dagg

When the first minyma started, Tjikalyi, Nyukana, and Tjikalyi's sister, we learned from them: 'Ai, walka wiru!', we copy them.

White fella did not make us draw!

Minyma nganmanyitja tjutangku tjaatarira Tjikalyilu Nyukanalu Tjikaliku kangkurungku tjana palyaningi kala tjanala nguru nyakula nintiringangi walka nyanga wiru tjutaku munuya arkara nintiringangi tjanala nguru.

Piranpa tjutangkula nganintintja wiyatu walka nyangaku.

Dora Haggie

I learnt the design in school when I visited Ernabella coming from Areyonga.

Walka nyangakuna nintiringu kuulangka Anapalala Utjulanguru pitjala.

Alison Curley

I went to the craftroom after school and Yanyi Baker showed me the design and I wove it into a rug. I didn't paint it.

Kuulangka malangkana anu craftroomakutu kani Yanyi Bakerlu nintiningi walka nyangatja kana nintiringkula rug-palyanu paintamilantja wiyana.

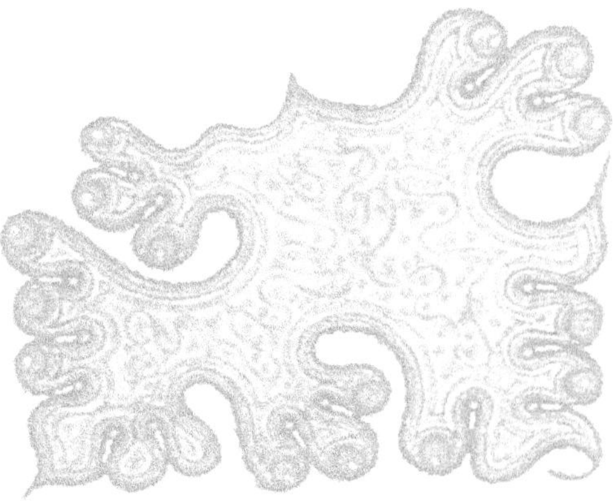

Traditional sand drawings

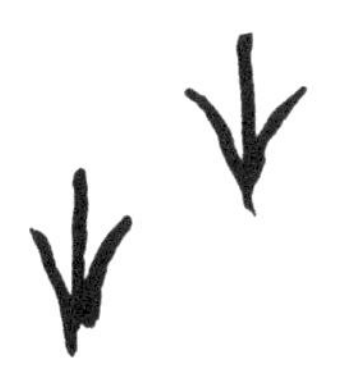

Kangaroo tracks/
malu tjina

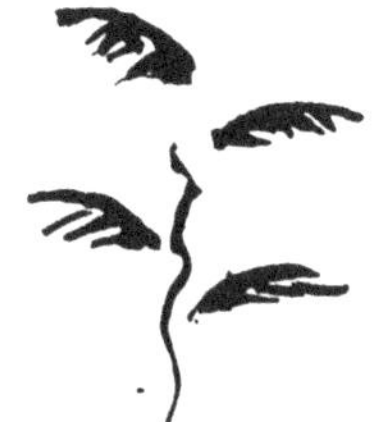

Perentie lizard tracks/
ngintaka tjina

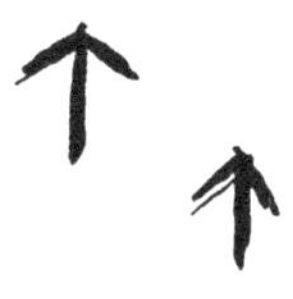

Emu tracks/
kalaya tjina

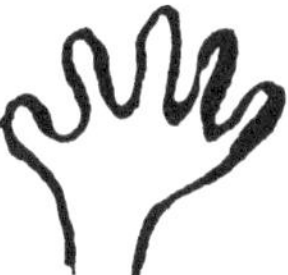

Hand/
mara

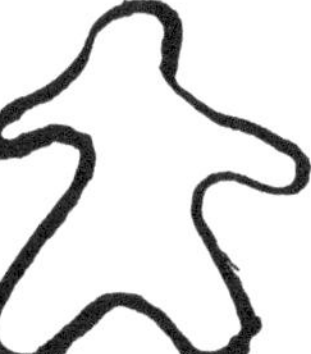

Shadow (around a person)/wiltja

Mission school

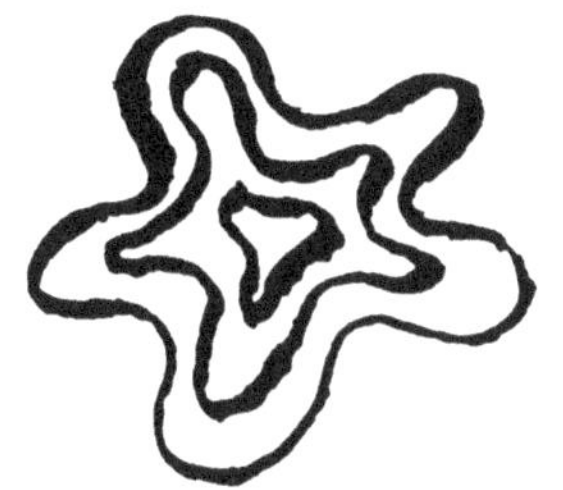

First schoolchildren's drawings on paper, not made in the sand before/ tjitjiku walka kuulangka, irititja mulapa wiya

Categories of designs as demonstrated by three artists, Tjimpuna Dunn, Kanytjupai Armstrong and Margaret Dagg, and confirmed by Nyukana Baker (sketches made by Ute Eickelkamp from drawings in the sand, see following pages)

Craftroom (drawing, painting)

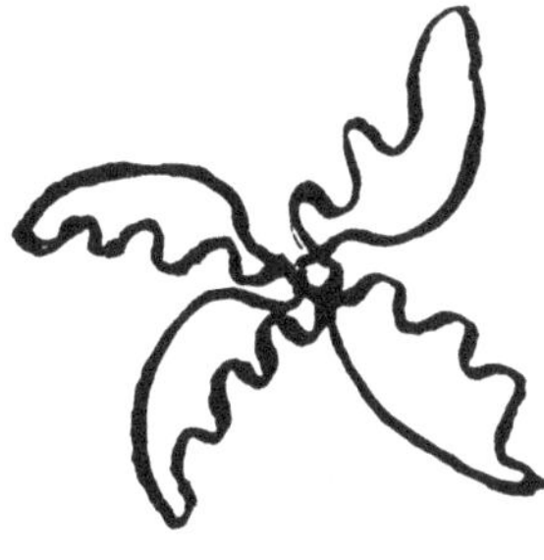

First craftroom design/
walka kura

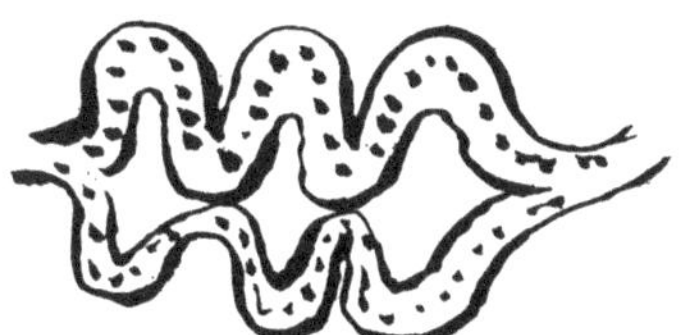

Improved design version/
walka wiruringu

Woodcarving/Punu

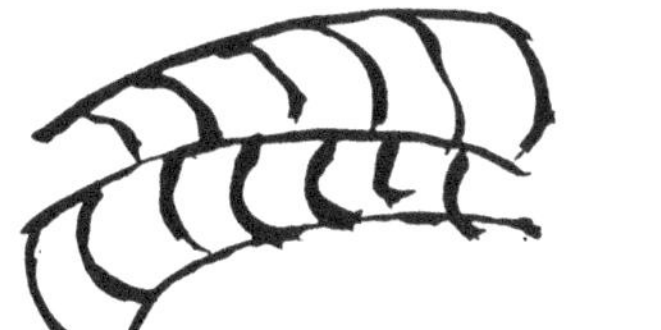

Two versions of early punu designs/
punuku walka irititja

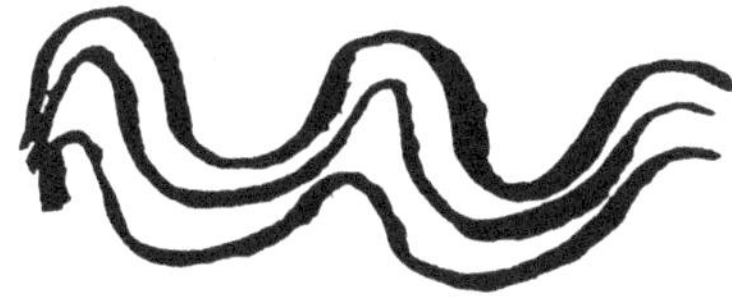

Improved punu design/
punuku walka wiruringu

Lucy Lester

First, I saw those in school, kids were doing it. I looked, and I was going to do it my own way, to start doing it, something a little bit different, you know?

We was all doing different designs, but the same way of putting it, like a circle, because in our society, Aboriginal way, we don't have corners. Just natural, I suppose, from our people, like how we make a wiltja.

Someone just started the little design and put colours in it, and somebody else thought, I'll do mine. Everybody doing something else, different looking and getting better and better every year and putting it on the mats and the floor rugs.

But many people ask, 'What's the story, what does it mean?', and we just say, 'Just designs, I'll be doing a design. There is this colour I like . . .'

The women created something better for themselves to be proud of, and it became more and more.

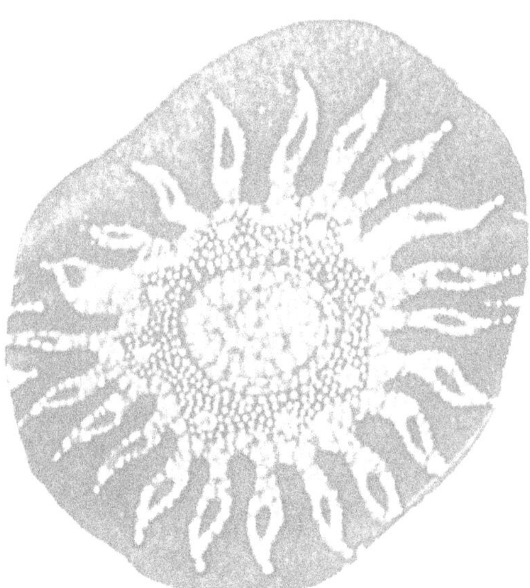

Kuwaripatjara, ngayulu nyangu schoolala, tjitji tjutangku walka tjunkunytjala. Ngayulu nyakula kulinu, ngayulu kuwari walkatjunanyi, ngayuku walka, walka kutjupa nguwan.

Palu nganana kutjulingku walka kutjupa kutjupa tjunangi, palu kutjuli manguri manguritjara. Panya ananguku arangka nganana corner kanyintja wiya, panya tjakangka anangu nganampa tjuta nguru wiltja palyara nintiringu.

Kutjupangku walkatjunu munu colour tjunu, ka kutjupangku kulinu, ngayulu ngayuku walkatjunkuku. Ka tjutangku kutjupa palyani, ka walka kutjupa mulapa ngaranyi munu wiruringanyi year kutjupa year kutjupa, munu matangka floor rugangka tjunanyi.

Palu tjutangku tjapilpai, 'Ka tjukurpa nyaa, ara nyaa wangkanyi?', ka nganana wangkapai, 'Walka kutjupa kutjupa. Ka ngayulu walkatjunangi munu colour tjunangi mukuringkula . . .'

Minyma tjutangku walka tjananku wiru kulira kananykananytju tjunu, ka ara tjana kulintja pulkaringu munu tjutaringu.

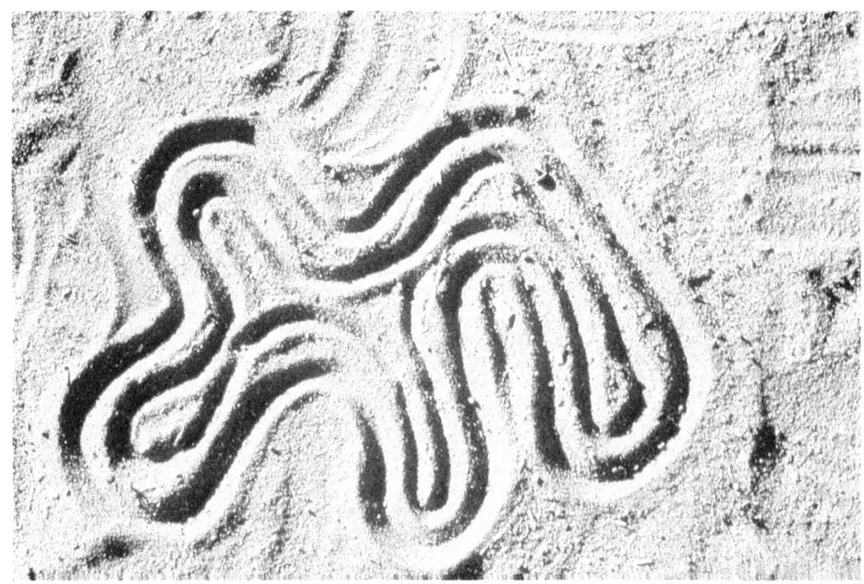

First schoolchildren's drawings
(photograph Ute Eickelkamp)

Early craftroom design
(photograph Ute Eickelkamp)

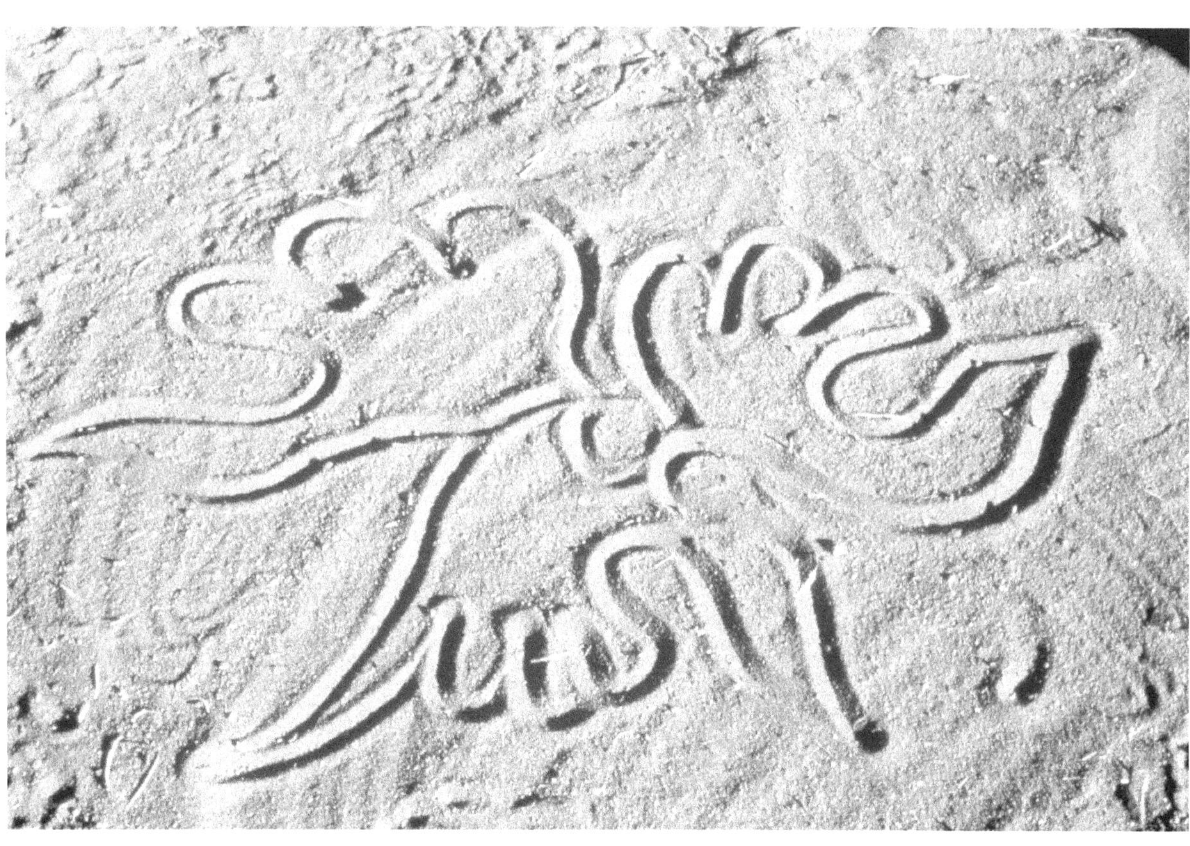

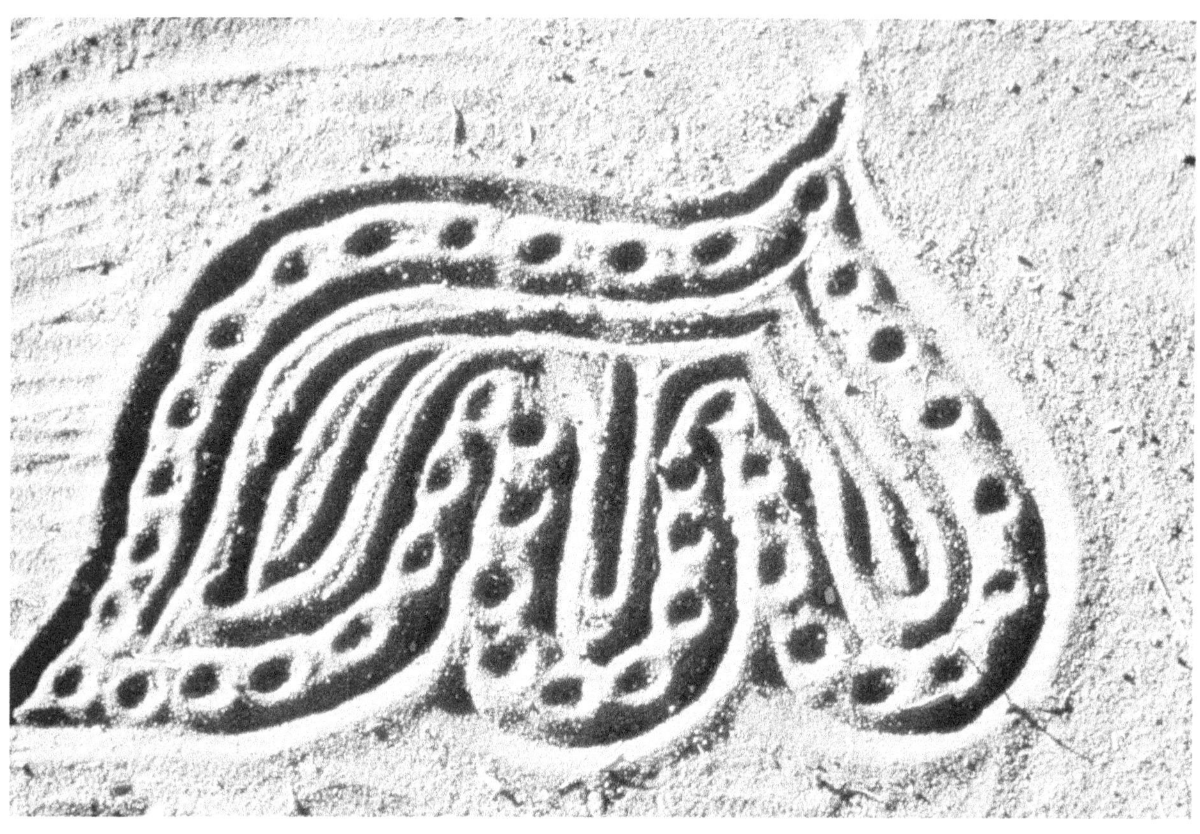

Improved craftroom design
(photograph Ute Eickelkamp)

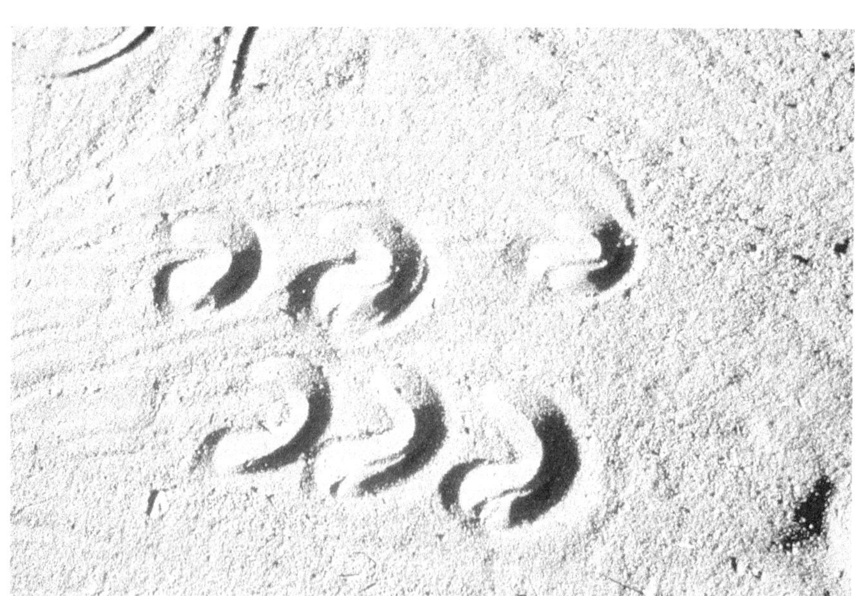

Early woodcarving design
(photograph Ute Eickelkamp)

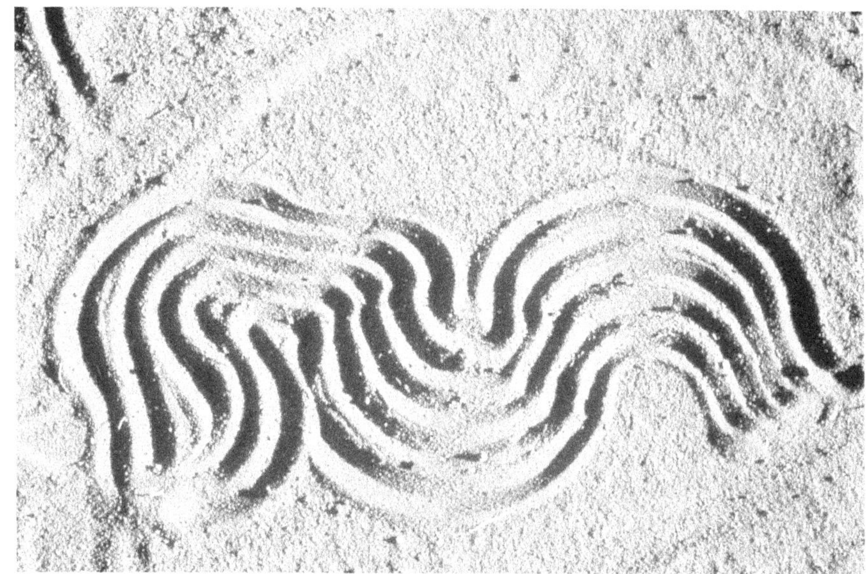

Improved woodcarving design (photograph Ute Eickelkamp)

Early woodcarving design (photograph Ute Eickelkamp)

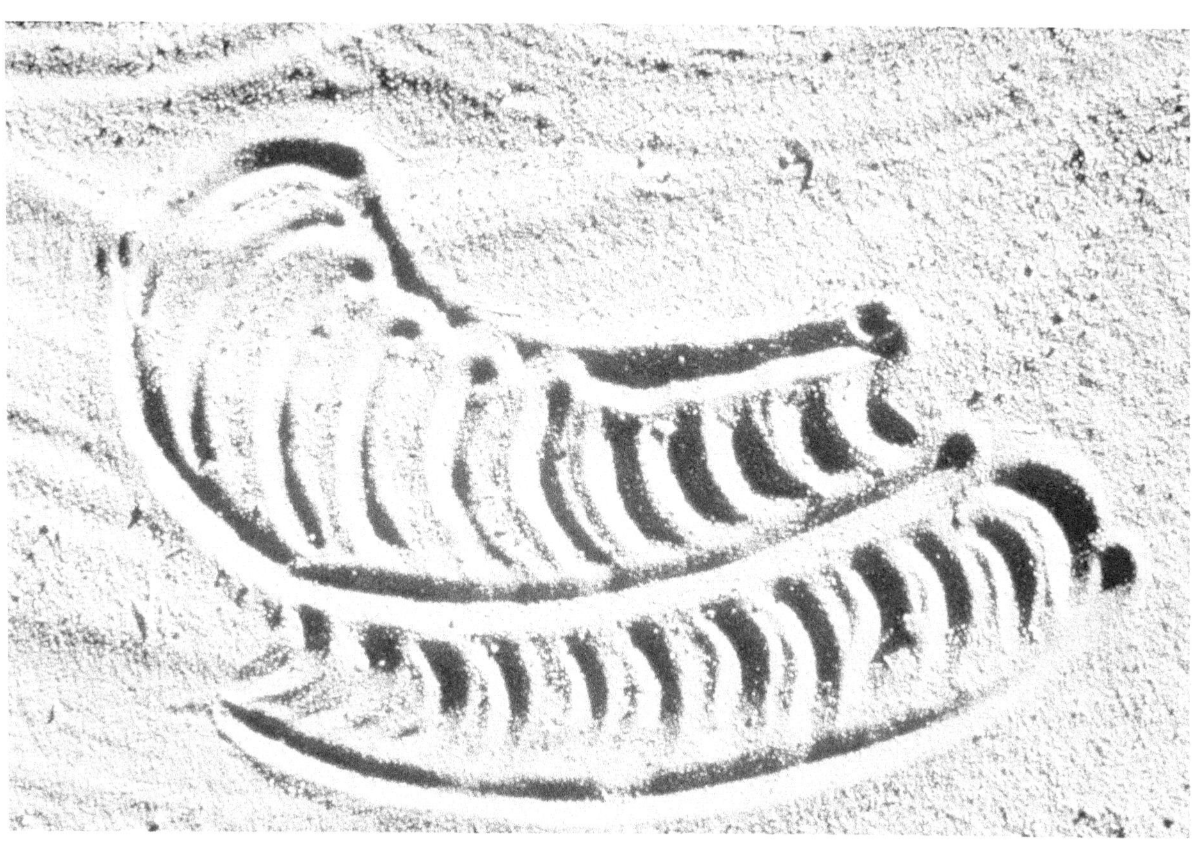

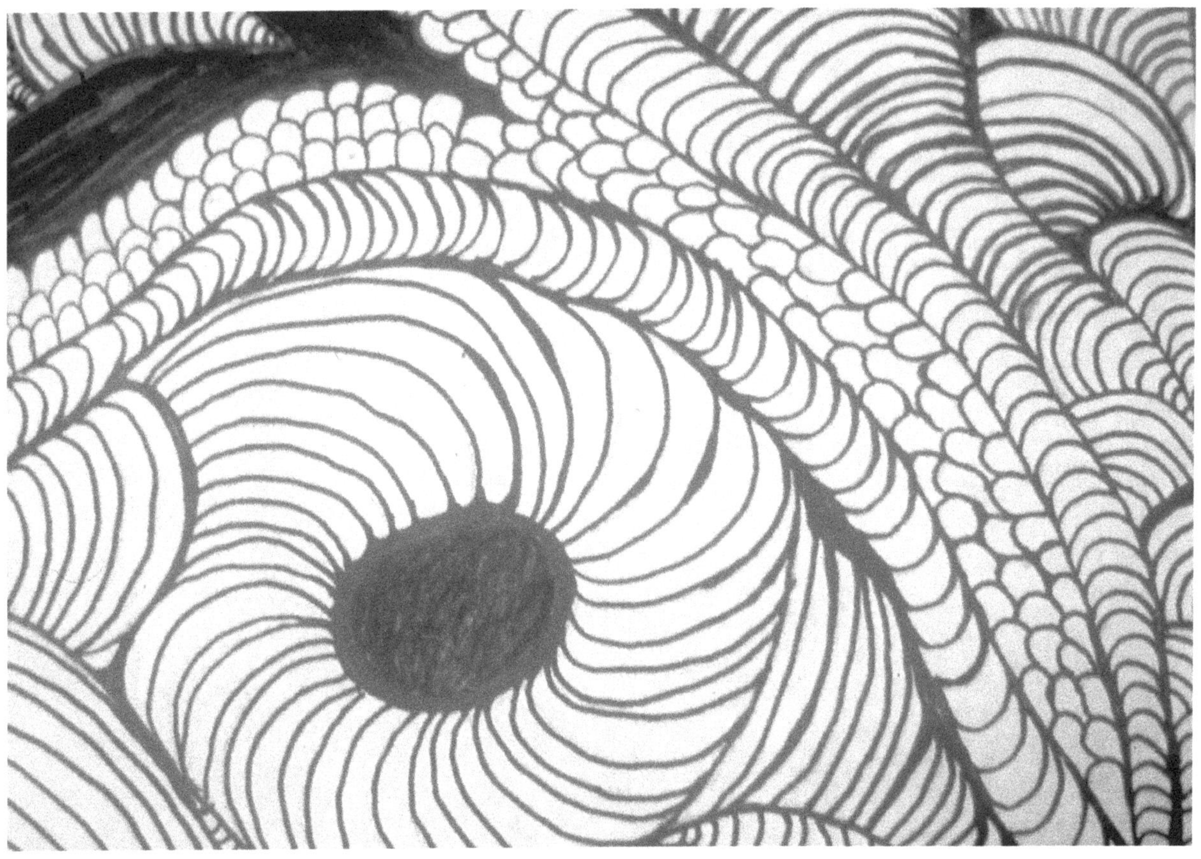

Punu design, by
Tjulkiwa Kunmanara, 1996,
artist's sketch on paper for
screenprint (the decorative
pattern used in woodcarving
has only recently been
produced on paper) (Ernabella
Arts collection, photograph
Ute Eickelkamp)

5

our lives as artists
nganampa ara: walka tjutatjara

ANGKALIYA (TULAPA) PURAMPI
ANGKALIYAKU TJUKURPA

(With Margaret Dagg, transcription by the Institute for Aboriginal Development, translation Ute Eickelkamp and Kanytjupai Armstrong)

Nganana kuulangka nyinapai mungawinki munula dinnerngka malangka wiyaringkupai munula ankupai kukaku Irupulainalakutu tangkiyingka munula kukatjanu malaku pitjapai mungartjikutu kampurarpa kulu mantjintjatjanu. Munu nganana kuulangka malangka Saturday ankupai kuula wiyaringkula Donalds Wellalakutu munu Wintuwintutjaralakutu kampurarpaku tangki tjutatjara. Munula Saturday Sunday ma nyinapai palu Anapalala ngurula unytju ankupai munu kutjupa ara mungartji malaku pitjapai kungkawara tjuta tjitji pulka tjutala ankupai munula homeland tjutangka ma ngaripai, homeland wiya palu shepherd tjutaku tjipi kanyilpai tjutaku ngurangka.

Margaretalu: Ka ngunytju mamangku tjipi tjuta kanyilpai iriti Shirley Wellala?

We went to school in the morning and finished at noon, when we would ride on donkeys out to Aeroplane to go hunting for game and to collect witchetty grubs and bush-tomatoes, and we'd return in the late afternoon. On Saturdays, after school, we all rode to Donalds Well or Wintuwintu to gather bush-tomatoes. So we didn't stay in Ernabella over weekends, but all the young women and older children went out to the homelands, which were sheep camps in those days.

Margaret: And your parents were shepherding at Shirley Well then?

As a young woman, but still going to school, I had some training in the clinic together with my older sister. I worked in hospital for two years after I had finished school and then I took

Ka kuula wiyaringkula ngayulu kungkawara tjukutjuku kuulitja clinicangka warkaringi munu nintiringi ngali kutjara paluru kungkawara pulkatu. Ka ngayulu kuula wiyaringkula haspitalangka warkaringi tjukutjuku ngayulu warkaringi mununa yiya kutjara wiyaringkula piruku warka kutjupangka ngayulu bakeringka warkaringi kungkawaralta breadala pauningi panya anangu community winkiku. Mununa palulanguru bakery wiyaringu munu warka kutjupangka piruku warkaringu craftroomangkalta. Mununa ngayuku katja number one mantjinu craftroomangka warkarira munu ngayulu warka wantintja wiya warkaringi alatjitu.

Tjaatarirana palyanu craftroomangka floor rug munula weavemilalpai kulu kulu nganalu Miss Bairdalulanya nintiningi rugakaku munu weavemilantjaku munu, nyaa, tjinaku panya malu miringuru palyantjaku paluru winkiku ngananya nintiningi. Miss Hilliardalulanya nintinu floor rug palyantjaku munu weavemilantjaku kulu nyara paluru tjanaya ngarangi. Uwa, tjukurpa nyangatjana ngayulu wangkangi.

Margaretalu: Munu panya nyuntu paint kulu walkatjunkupai mulapa?

Painting paperangka kulu ngarapai paper munu panangka kulu kulula walkatjunkupai. Ngayuku walkana nyangatja walkatjunanyi alatji alatjila palyalpai. Rugala nyanga palu purinypa palyalpai.

up another job in the bakery, where the young women were making bread for the whole community. I left the bakery to commence work in the craftroom and I had my first son then, whom I took with me to the craftroom. I didn't stop working when I had my children.

The craftroom began with the women making floor rugs and weaving, taught by Miss Baird, and we also made leather shoes from kangaroo skin with her. Then Miss Hilliard supervised the rug and shoe-making as well as weaving, yes, this is how I remember it.

Margaret: And you also did painting?

We painted on paper and we also made sand drawings. This is how I create my design.

The designs on rug were similar to this.

Margaret: Her design is easily recognisable since it resembles Nyukana's design. Maybe white people can't see that and try to identify it in vain, and only Pitjantjatjara people have a trained eye.

Yes, we painted that design at school and I also create it in batik now.

The spun wool was dyed in hot water: we had to light a fire under a drum to boil the water and poured in the dye. A lot of wool was dyed in this way and we made rugs for sale (with the money going back into the craftroom). When a rug was finished, we would dye some more wool to create the design in different colours again.

Margaretalu: Palumpa walka mulapa uti ngurkatankunytjaku tjukutjuku nyaranyi Nyukanaku walka purunypa. Palu tjinguru piranypa kutjupa tjuta ninti wiya munu putu ngurkantankupai walka Pitjantjatjara tjutaku tjana kutju ninti.

Uwa, kuulangka nganana walkatjunkupai walka palapalunya munu kuwari kulu ngayulu batikingka walkatjunkupai. Ngayulu craftroomangka warkarira kana palulanguru ngayulu warkarinyi wantinytja wiya.

Munula wuul dyemilalpai nganana nyangangka mina waruntjaku ngarapai ka nganana waru tjunkupai unngu dyemilantjikitjangku munu nganana dyemilalpai wuul tjuta munu nganana rugka palyalpai manikitjangku munula palyara wiyaringkula piruku kutjupa ngapartji boilamilalpai dye, walka kutjupa palyantjikitjangku. Munu nganana rugangka palyalpai munu weavemilalpai dyemilantjatjanungku malangka.

Margaretalu: Uwa, tjana mulapa floor rug weaving tjutakulu palyalpai nyanga purunypa tjukutjuku, wuul tjana rungkalpai tjukutjuku mulapa ka palula malangka kalarmilalpai munula paltjilpai munu kilinankupai munu dyengka tjunkupai kalaringkunytjaku ka palula malangka piltiringkupailta kaya katalpai.

Ka nganana kuwari nguwanpalta Win Hilliardanya nyinantja arangka nganana batiki palyanu munula nyara palula ara batiki palyara nintiringangi munu batikingka piruku palyaningi. Walka panya palunyatu.

Munu palulanguru ngayulu warka nyara palula warkarinytjatjanu anu ngura kutjupakutu, Japanalakutu warkaku. Win Hilliardanya ngali

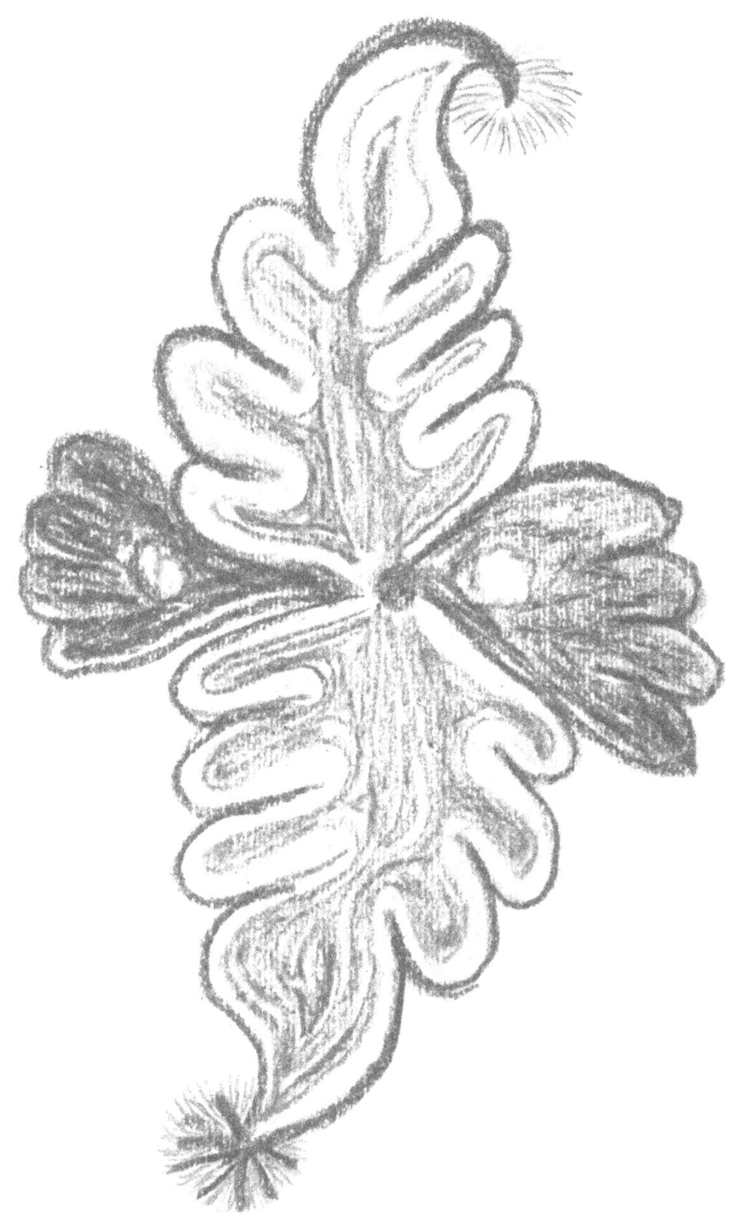

Angkaliya's design
(Ute Eickelkamp collection)

anu batik exhibitionku punu kulu palyantjkitja Panmanya kutjutjarala anu. Munu ngayulu pitjangu mununa anu warka kutjupa kutu anangu kutjupa tjuta Cedunala warka nyanga ngura nyara palunya palyantjikitja. Anangu panya ngurpa tjutala nintiningi.

Margaretalu: Uwa, nganana batik palyaningi munu nintiningi anangu kutjupa tjuta.

Mununa piruku palulanguru pitjangu mununa tjukutjuku warkaringi mununa palulanguru piruku anu Wupatintakutu anu mununa nyara palula warkaringi mununa malaku pitjangu mununa pikatjarаringuna mununa pikatjararingkula warka nyara palunya wantintja wiya.

Mununa kuwari nyanga warkarinyitu homelandangka craftroomanguru ngayulu pakanu munu ngayuku craftroom tjunu tjitangka kana warkarinyi. Holidayngka kutju ngayulu warkaringkupai panya weekendangka Saturday Sunday kutju panya ngayuku warka kutjara bakery munu craftroom. Ngayuku untalpa kulu paluru kuulangka warkaringi munu weekend warkaringkupaitu.

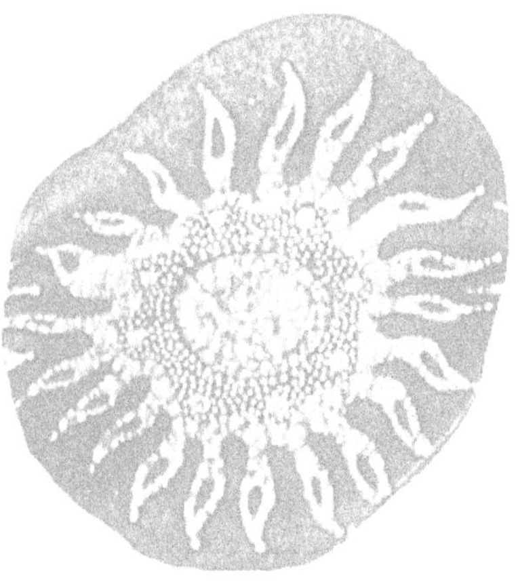

Margaretalu: Nyura warka nyangatja ngura kutjupangka nyangu munu nintiringu?

Wiya warka nyanga palunyala nganana warara tjartamilanu Anapalala

Margaret: Yes, the wool was spun into a fine thin thread, it was coloured and washed and dyed again, then hung out to dry. It could then be woven into a rug, which was completed by cutting the loose ends of the threads to an even edge.

And some time after Win Hilliard had been the craft adviser, batik was introduced. We learnt the batik technique (in a workshop at Ernabella) and we have been creating this design in batik ever since.

Just after we had started batik, I travelled to Japan to do some work there. Win Hilliard and I went to an exhibition of batik, and woodcarving was demonstrated by Sandy, who was with us. I came back home and left again for Ceduna, where I conducted a batik workshop to teach Anangu from other places in this medium.

Margaret: Yes, they demonstrated batik and passed on their knowledge to other Anangu.

Again, I returned to Ernabella to work for a short while before I went to Warburton, where I also worked. When I came back from there, I fell ill, but I would nevertheless go to the craftroom.

Nowadays, I have my own studio on my homeland. We set up a shed where I can work on Saturdays and Sundays, or during holidays. I have another job in the bakery. My daughter works at school and she joins me in the craftroom on weekends.

Margaret: Didn't you all go to another place to watch and learn?

minyma pirantulanya nintinu warka nyanga palunya floor rug palyatjaku weavemilantjaku munu wuul (inyu) rungkatjaku. Mayawaranya Nura Rupertanya munu Mayawaranya wiyaringu munu Nyingutanya weavemilalpai ninti. Nyingutanya munuya nyara Fregonta nyinanyi kutjupa tjuta munu Amatala nyinanyi. Anapalala kutjungkala nintiringu nganana uwankaraya anu Anapalala kutjunguru.

No, our work grew in Ernabella, where it started when a white woman came and taught us how to make woven floor rugs and how to spin wool for that purpose. Mayawara and Nura Rupert were the first to make floor rugs and when Mayawara dropped out, Nyinguta learnt weaving, Nyinguta and women who now live in Fregon and Amata.

Ernabella is the place where we all trained in craft. It all started in Ernabella.

Ute: Where do you buy your material?

Craftroomangka palu nganampa kuwari nyanganguru ordermilalpai ka pitjapai material tjuta craftroomakutu kala palyara katipai craftroomakutu munula tjalamilalpai.

Uwa palya.

Ute: Where do you buy your material nowadays?

I purchase it in the craftroom, where it is ordered and sent to, and I also sell my work to the craftroom.

Alright? I finish here.

MARGARET DAGG
MARGARETAKU TJUKURPA

(Written and translated by the artist)

I was born just southwest of Ernabella as the fourth child. My parents came from out west, they lived here in Ernabella all their lives. That's where I grew up, and spent my first school years here in Ernabella. Miss Nicholson was my teacher and she taught me in my own language, which has helped me a lot in my work as a translator.

My family then moved to Fregon, where I continued my schooling. After lunch we were sent to homes for domestic duties as work experience. That is where I met Kanytjupai and she became my best friend. We

Ngayulu iti ngaringu Ernabellala itingka ka ngayuku mama ngunytju ngura nyangatja ngurara wiya panya paluru pula pitjangu ngura wilureranguru palu wilurara pararinguru wiya nyanga ilanguru munu paluru pula nyangangka alatjitu nyinara pamparingkula tjilpiringu ngura nyanga Ernabellala. Ka ngayulu nyanga palula tjitji pulkaringu mununa kulangka tjatarira tjarpangu nyanga palula. Ka ngayuku teacher Miss Nicholsonnga mununi paluru wirungku nintinu wangka pitjanytjatjaraku ngayuku wangkaku kana nyara palulanguru ngayulu

continued to work together in Fregon after I finished my schooling. It was in Mrs Fletcher's house. We did the cleaning every morning, as in doing the dishes, making the beds, sweeping the floors, washing the clothes and hanging them out to dry before we sat down for a cup of tea outside. The next job would be to do the vegetables for lunch, then we went off to have lunch with our own relations. After lunch we returned to continue the work, washing dishes and saucepans. This was a Monday to Friday job and we were paid a little bit of money, which we spent on food for the weekend. We sometimes came in on the weekend just to help with the dishes only.

On weekends we would go out hunting for rabbits with other women. We spent the rest of the weekends out bush. We learn a lot of our culture when we are children. Other things we learned from our relations were how to make wiltja, how to get witchetty

Margaret Dagg in the craftroom at Fregon, 1968 (photograph Dudley Dagg)

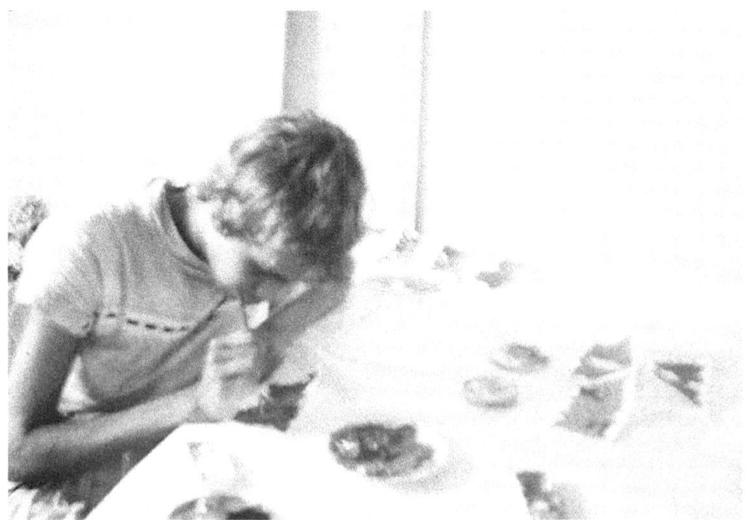

nintiringkunytjatjanungku tjukurpa walkatjunkupai.

Ka ngula ngayuku mama ngunytju ngura nyangatja wantikatira anu Fregontakutu kana nyara palula piruku kulangka tjarpangi. Panya kulitjana anu nyanganguru kalanya tinangka malangka wali tjuta kutu iyalpai warkarira nintiringkunytjaku. Kana ngula nyara palula Kanytjupainya nyangu ka paluru ngayuku malparingu, munu paluru ngali nyara palula tjungu warkaripai panya ngayulu kula wiyaringkula ngulalta. Mrs Fletcherku walingkali warkaripai. Ngali rawa warkaku pitjapai tjintu uwankarangka munuli pulita tjuta paltjilpai, munu pita tjuta palyalpai, floor sweepamilalpai, munu ulytja tjuta paltjira utitjunkupai piltiringkunytjaku kapati tjikintja kuwaripangka. Munuli palulanguru kapatingka malangka mai ukiri tjutalta kutjalpai tjanampa paluru tjana lunch ngalkunytjaku, munuli ngali ankupai ngalimpa walytja tjutangka mai ngalkunytjikitja. Munuli palulanguru maingka malangka pitjapai tjana panya mai ngalkunytja kilinankunytjikitja pulita tjuta saucepan tjuta kulu kulu. Warka nyanga alatjili rawangku palyalpai Mondaynguru Fridaykutu munuli mani tjukutjuku mantjilpai munu payamilalpai mai Saturdayku munu Sundayku. Kutjupa arali pitjapai Saturdayngka munu Sundayngka tjana panya mai ngalkunytja pulitja tjuta kutju paltjira alpamilantjikitja.

Munu wiki kutjupangka nganana rapitaku ankupai minyma kutjupa tjutangka tjungu, munula kutjupa ara ma nyinapai putingka kukaku ankula munula mungartji kutju pitjapai. Nganana nganampa ara tjutaku nintiringu tjitji tjukutjukulpi.

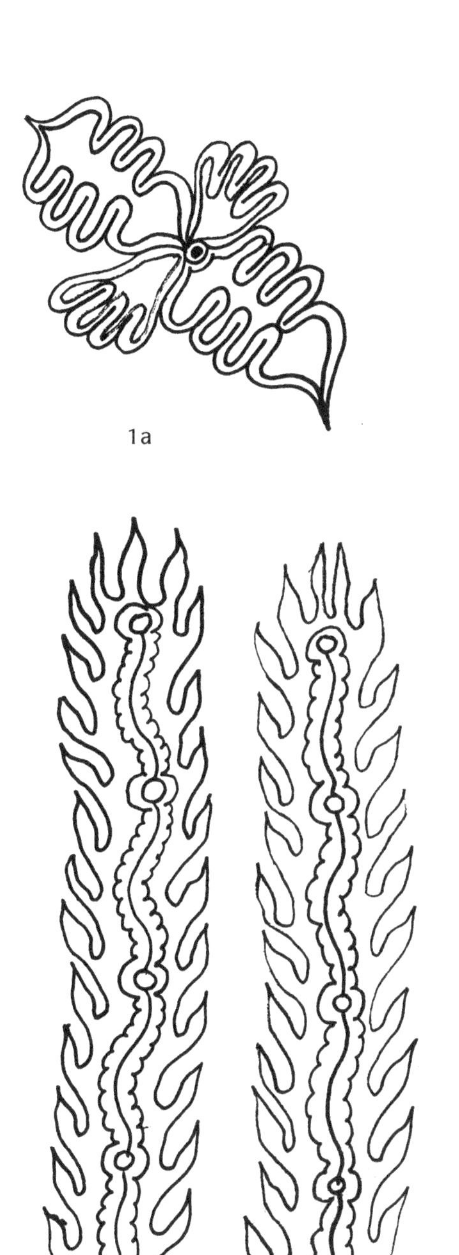

1a

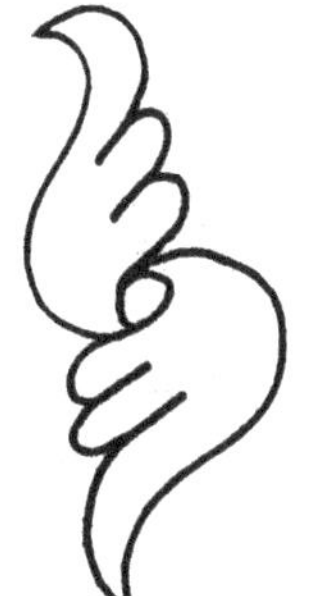

1b

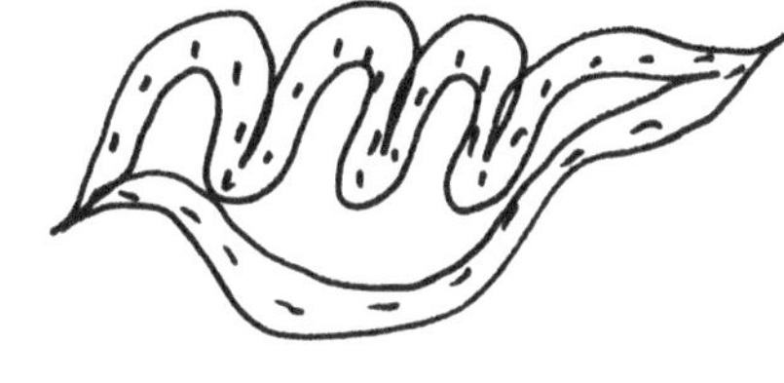

1c

Margaret's illustration of a selection of her designs, coloured pencil on paper, 1995 (Ute Eickelkamp collection)

Selection of design elements by Margaret Dagg

1. Designs developed during her years at the craftroom in Fregon
 a. painted on small cards
 b. painted on bookmarks
 c. improved design used in miniature paintings

2. A major design used in the batik medium. The artist commences the creation with the circles, then connects these with a line which is then bracketed by curvy lines on either side. The design is finally completed with the flame-like outer line.

3, 4 and 5. Various other designs from Margaret's repertoire, which is ever-increasing, with new combinations of her developed design elements providing scope for innovation while her individual style is maintained.

2

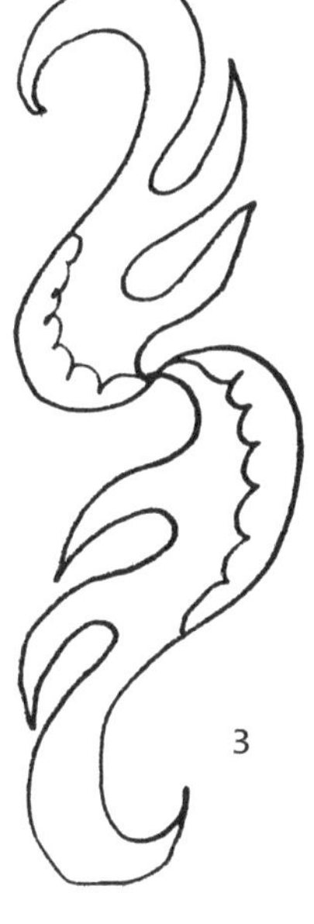

3

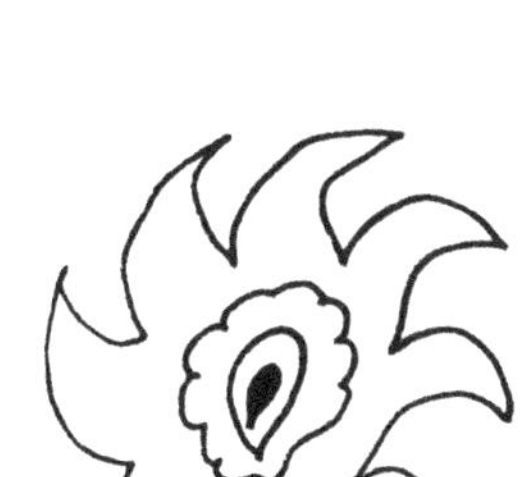

4

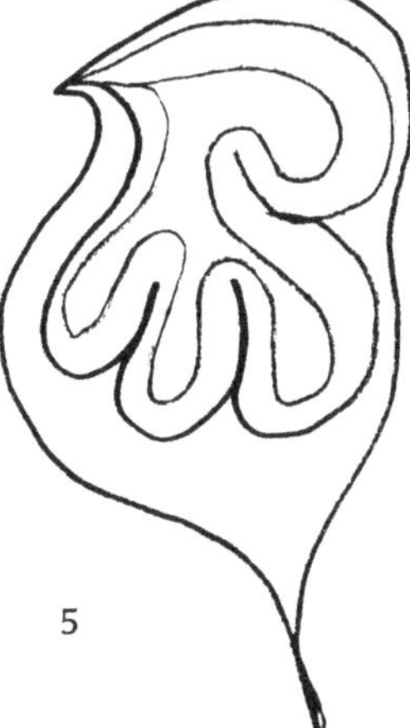

5

grubs and honeyants, and collect wild tomatoes, bush-onions, and many other fruits in the wild.

My job was interesting in the beginning but I grew tired of doing the same thing all the time. So I disappeared for a while for a holiday and when I came back I decided to do a different job.

I went to work in the craftroom, where I started to paint small cards in watercolours and moccasins with designs in oils. Other women would sew the moccasins, which were cut out of kangaroo skins, together. I learned all the crafts from the other women and I still do many of them as a hobby. Win Hilliard was the manager and teacher of the craftroom.

And now I live just outside of Ernabella, where my house has a room just for craft.

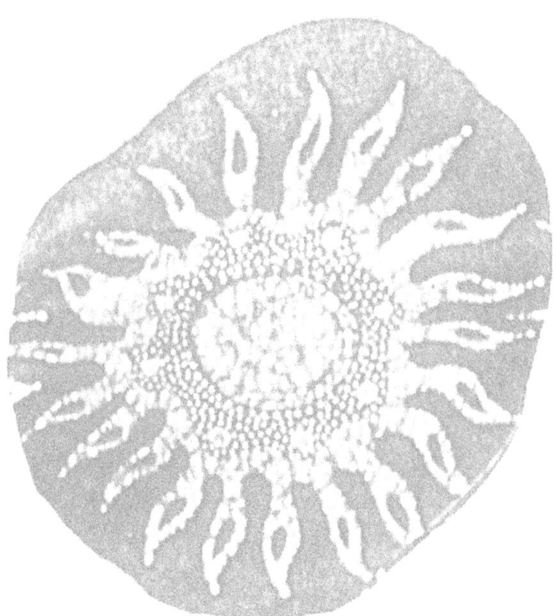

Munula kutjupa tjutaku kulu nintiringu nganampa ngunytjunguru munu kutjupa tjutanguru kulu. Wiltja palyantjaku walytjangku munu maku mantjintjaku tjala tjawantjaku, kampurarpa mantjintjaku munu tjanmata mantjintjaku, munu mai putitja kutjupa tjuta kulu.

Uwa ngayulu nganmanypa warkaku mukuringangi palu ngulana ma pakuringu warka kutjungka rawa, warkarira warkarira. Kana palulanguru ankupai alatai mununa malaku pitjala kulinu warka kutjupangka warkarinytjikitjangku.

Mununa palulanguru anu craftroomangka warkarinytjikitja. Mununa nyara palula warkarira ngayulu cards kulunypa tjutangka paintamilalpai Anapalaku walka, munu oil colourngka walkatjunkupai walka moccassinta. Minyma kutjupa tjutangkuya nganmanytju walkatjura katalpai munuya wakara wiyara tjunkupai kala nganana malangka walka palyalpai. Ngayulu warka nyanga palumpa nintiringu minyma kutjupa tjuta nyakula nyakula, munu ngayulu kuwari warka nyanga palunya tjananya walytjangku kanyini mununa rawangku palyalpai. Win Hilliardanya nyangangka nyinangi iriti nintilpai munu craftroomaku mayatja.

Ka ngayulu kuwari Anapalala nyinanyi palu tjukutjuku patu nguwanpa ka ngayuku walingka craftroom tjukutjuku ngaranyi ngayulu warkarinytjku.

MARIE WARREN
MARIEKU TJUKURPA

(Written by Marie in Ernabella, 1996)
(Translation by Nura Ward, proofreading by Kanytjupai Armstrong)

I came from Marree, and I lived on our grandfather's cattle station called Finniss Springs. So when the Ghan stopped shunting through Marree, my mother, Nancy Dodd, moved to Port Augusta. While living in Port Augusta, I didn't get on with my mother.

After all the trouble I ran away from home and I lived on the streets in Adelaide, down the River Torrens with the other street kids, for about one and a half years. This happened when I was twelve and a half years old.

After all that I met my children's father and I came to live in Ernabella, and I ended up working at Ernabella Arts in 1991. I was taught how to do silk printing and went on to doing screenprinting. I have been doing all of the colour ways for Ernabella Arts since then.

I don't live in Ernabella, but I live in Mintabie at the moment. When Ernabella Arts needs any work done I will go over and do all the printing for them.

I love screenprinting so much that I am hoping to get my own business going in screenprinting in the near future.

But I will never forget about all the years with Ernabella Arts in which it was a privilege to work there. If it wasn't for them I wouldn't know where or how I would have survived.

Nganmanypa ngayulu pitjangu Marreelanguru mununa nyinangi ngayuku tjamuku ngurangka ngura pulukaku ngura paluru ini Finniss Springsnya. Ka traina ankunytja wiyaringu Marreela ka ngayuku ngunytju Nancy Doddanya anu Port Augustalakutu palu ngayulu ngunytjula tjungu ankunytja wiya palu troublela pulka wirkanu malangka.

Kana nyara palula ara anu Adelaidalakutu mununa karu panya Torrensala itingka nyinangi tjitji kutjupa tjutangka tjunguringkula yiya kutju nguwanpa nyangatjana kungkawara tjukutjuku alatjiringi twelve yiya nguwanpa nyinara.

Nyangangka malangka ngayulu kuritjararingu mununa tjitji mantjinu mununa anu Anapalalakutu. Mununa wakaringi craftroomangka Anapalala 1991ta. Ngayulu nintiringangi walkaku mununa walkatjunangi Kuwari ngayulu kutjupa kutjupa palyani.

Palu ngayulu nyinanyi Anapalala wiya Mintabaila kuwari. Mununa ngalya pitjapai Anapalala wakarinytjikitja rawa.

Ngayulu pulkara mukuringanyi walka nyanga palumpa mununa nintiringangi waltjangku kanyintjikitja munu palyantjikitja.

Ngayulu watarkurintja wiya rawa pitjapai Anapalaku. Nyangatja warka wiru mulapa. Nganmanypana watarku nyinangi nyanganpa kulintja wiya mununa kuwari pulkara nintiringanyi mununa tjinguru nintilku anangu kutjupa tjuta Mintabaila.

MAKINTI MINUTJUKUR
MAKINTIKU TJUKURPA

I was born in Alice Springs in 1957 because my parents were working in church there. They brought me back to Ernabella as a baby, and when I grew older, I lived in a different place.

School years in Adelaide

My first schooling was here in Ernabella, and I learnt in Pitjantjatjara. A young woman, Miss Hill, spoke a lot of Pitjantjatjara, so she taught it and only very little English. But it was hard to learn, slowly, but Pitjantjatjara was quick. I read Pitjantjatjara, write Pitjantjatjara and speak Pitjantjatjara. But when I grew up – I was 12 or 13 years old – I started to learn English.

That time, my family wanted me to go to Adelaide to go to college or high school there. So they put me there for one year, and I was alone. There were no Anangu in the school, but I got a lot of friends there. Still, it was too hard for me to be alone.

I was very good at school and young for my class, and the teachers chose me to say that I was good in English. I was trying hard and so they gave me a certificate. I was also the only one from my class to be on a stage with other girls. That was at the end of school.

I stayed with friends who used to work in Ernabella when I was little. They were good friends, they looked after me and I lived with them.

Return to Ernabella – the craftroom

I came back to Ernabella at Christmas time. I was thinking, 'I don't want to go back', 'cause it was too hard. It was good to learn from a different life and different people.

When I finished school, I started working in the craftroom. Ernabella wasn't a mission anymore, and Win Hilliard was still the art adviser.

It was different from today: there were lots of women working, older women, younger women, and me. The craftroom has been important for the women. In the old days, mothers and daughters were working together. They all worked and we grew up in there, making art. And it is still important to keep that craftwork going.

The first designs

Maybe the Ernabella design is really a women's design. I saw an old video that shows Nungalka and Tjikalyi as children drawing these designs in the sand. It looked like this:

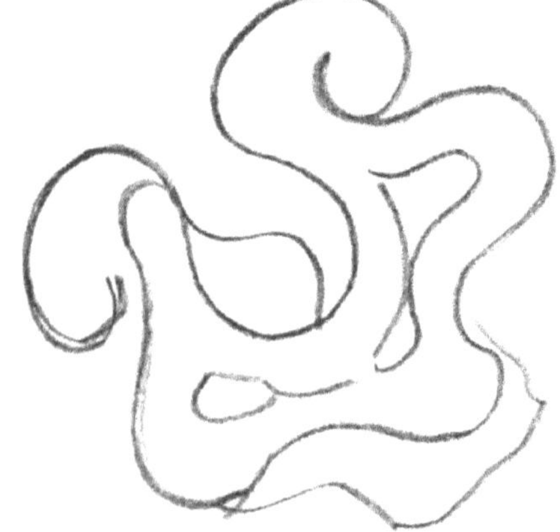

And the white man was saying, 'Ai, Nungalka, this is the first design!' They started in the sand first, and I thought, 'So, that's how it was'.

Perhaps they were all sitting together telling stories, doing walkatjunanyi and drawing the stories in the sand: making lines with three fingers to show rocks or a creek, drawing a semicircle with one finger for a person, a larger one for a wiltja, then short crossing lines as a campfire, and little filled-in circles showing spinifex grass and bushes. All this is shown as if looking from the top, from above. Then they went to school and there they made these drawings on paper, using chalk.

These first designs were different, pretty bad. They started with shapes different from today, maybe like this:

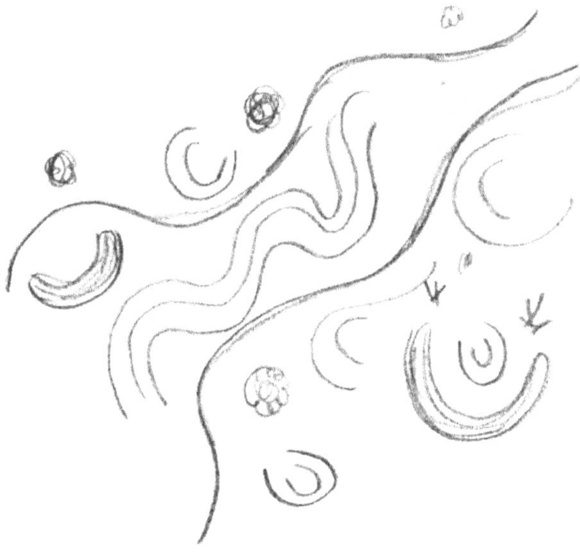

And they filled in colours – green, yellow – and discovered 'That's a beautiful design!'.

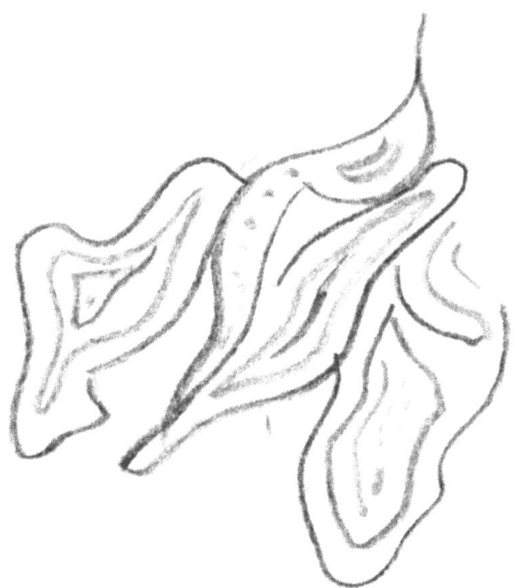

But today, they do it different:

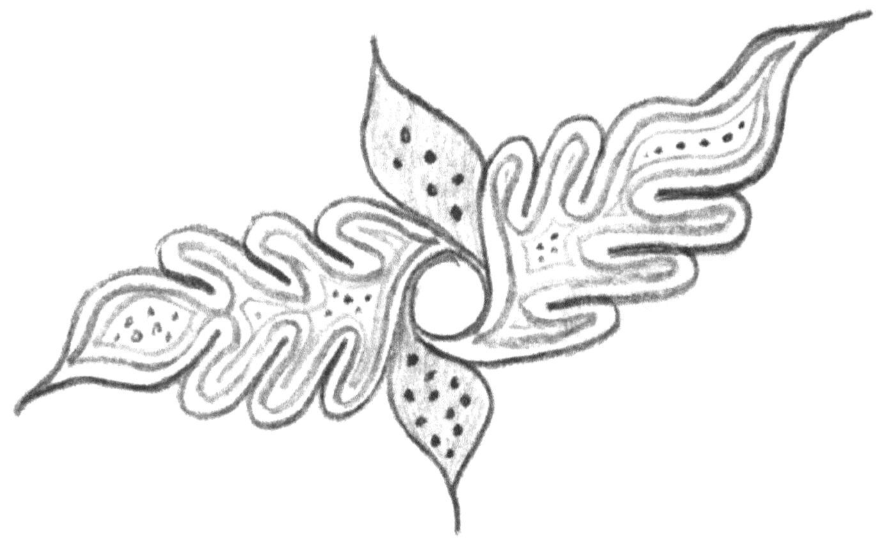

Pattern for cutting a moccasin (from the undated handwritten booklet by Winifred Hilliard,'General Information', Ernabella Arts collection)

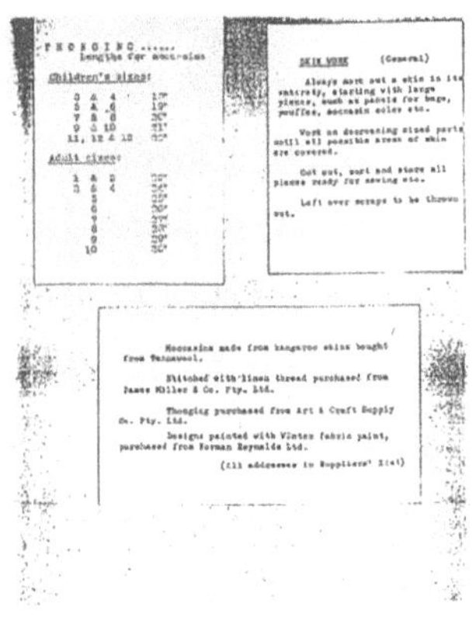

THONGING ......
Lengths for moccasins

Children's sizes:

3 & 4 17"
5 & 6 19"
7 & 8 [illegible]
9 & 10 [illegible]
11, 12 & 13 [illegible]

Adult sizes:

[illegible]

SKIN WORK (General)

Always sort out a skin in its entirety, starting with large pieces, such as panels for bags, pouffes, moccasin soles etc.

Work on decreasing sized parts until all possible areas of skin are covered.

Cut out, sort and store all pieces ready for sewing etc.

Left over scraps to be thrown out.

Moccasins made from kangaroo skins bought from Tanamool.

Stitched with linen thread purchased from James Miller & Co. Pty. Ltd.

Thonging purchased from Art & Craft Supply Co. Pty. Ltd.

Designs painted with Vinter fabric paint, purchased from Norman Reynolds Ltd.

(All addresses in Suppliers' list)

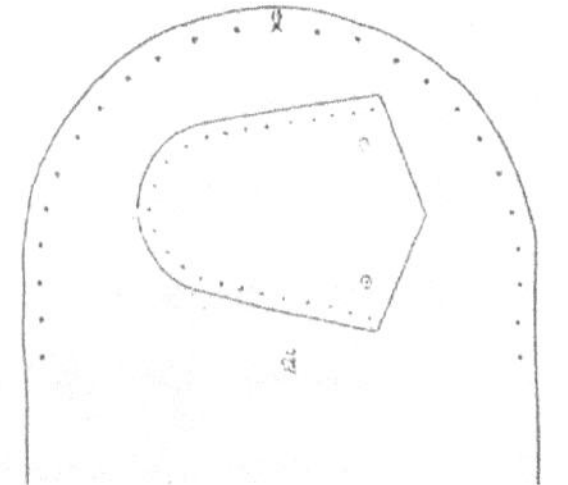

I was eight or nine years old when I first saw the women painting the design on moccasins made from kangaroo skins. The older women cut out the patterns in different sizes and sewed them up. A fur sole was put inside and they painted the design on the shoe.

Then I started to learn batik. My aunty Tjunkaya and Nyukana showed me; they all know. And I learnt and made beautiful designs on batik and canvas.

I also had the job of doing bookkeeping, filling in timesheets, and organising the payments. The men all had good jobs, but there was no other work for women in Ernabella. The craftroom kept us busy from Monday to Sunday.

The community today

At present, I am the chairperson of the Women's Council and was the mayor of Pukatja [Ernabella] until that position was cut by ATSIC [the Aboriginal and Torres Strait Islander Commission] in 1996. I am supervisor for CDOs [community development officers] now.

Community work is important for Anangu and also church is important for all the Christian people. We should have a strong church.

In mission times, a white man, Bill Edwards, was the superintendent. He runs two positions in the community: the money and work side, and the church – he was a reverend too. There were also Anangu church elders and they worked together on both sides.

Now it's different: people like the CDOs only run community business, and Christians work only for the church. It's good for Anangu to control, but I think, maybe it's too hard.

Perhaps the children need better education. Today, our children should learn for our future. They should go to school and to university, and when they have learnt they should come back to run the community, truly by Anangu.

LEXIE INGKATJI
LEXIEKU TJUKURPA

(Translation by Kanytjupai Armstrong)

I grew up in Ernabella where I went to school. Carol Williams was in my class; now she also paints on silk in the craftroom.

I came to the craftroom a short while ago and I started painting on canvas. Not stories about bushfood, just designs.

I don't think I will start batik, I like painting silk scarves. One lady came from Adelaide and we had a workshop to learn the technique. This is how you do it: first, you choose a piece of white silk and then it is pinned on a frame. The

Nyanga palulana pulkaringu Anapalala panya ngayulu schoolangka tjarpapai Carolta tjungu ka kuwari paluru ngalitu paintamilalpai silkangka craftroomangka.

Panya craftroomangka ngayulu warkaringu kuwari nguwanpa mununa paintamilalpai canvasangka mai putitjatjara wiya panya walka kutjula palyalpai.

Batikakuna ngurpa palu silka kutjuna paintamilalpai panya kungka piranpa kutju mungatu pitjangu Adelaidalanguru ngananyanya nintitjikitja nyanga alatjila palyaningi

Painted silk scarves, 1996 (Ernabella Arts collection, photograph Ute Eickelkamp)

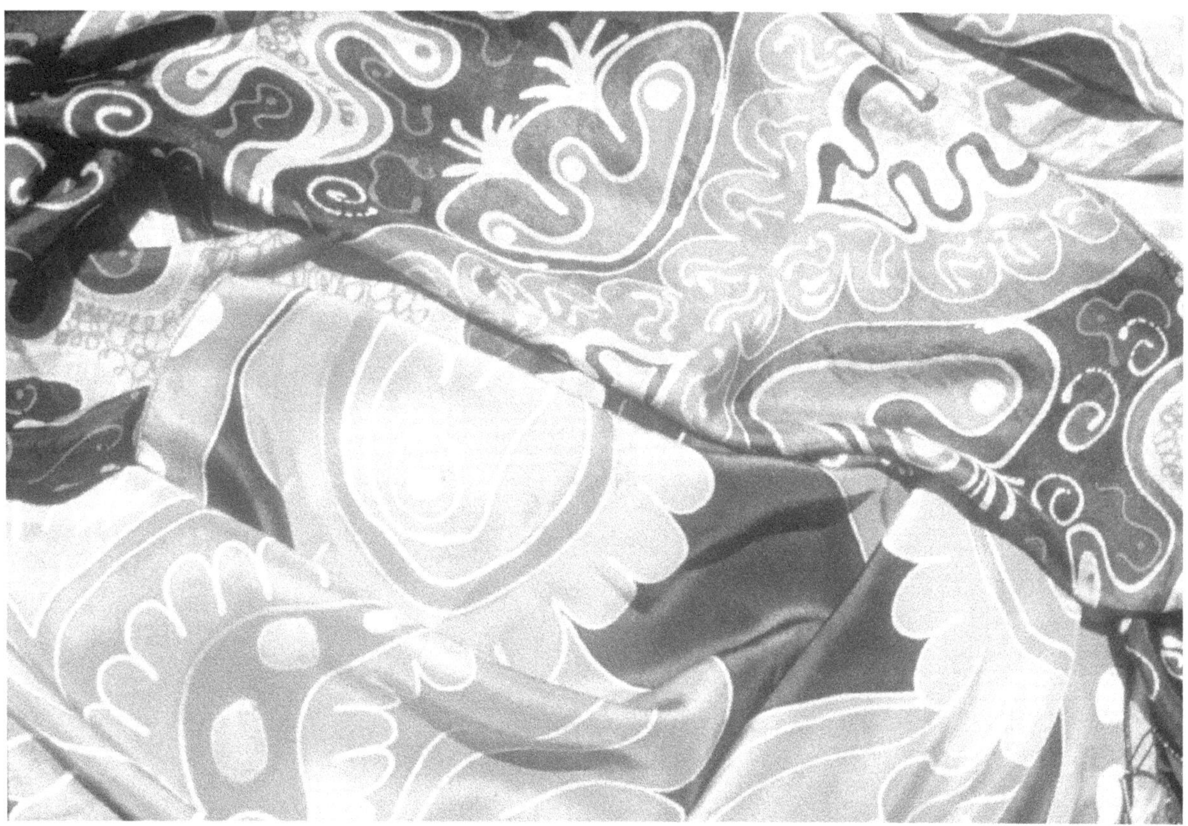

design is painted on the silk with gutta, using a little plastic bottle with a long neck. This stops the colour from running. Then, the colours are filled in with a paint brush. It dries quickly. It's finished now. Jenni [the art coordinator] will steam the scarf.

When I come to work at the craftroom, I bring my little son with me. My sister Yilpi also does silk painting here, as well as batik.

nganmanytjula raiki piranpa mantjira framengka tjakatjunangi munula walkatjunangi. Patala tjaa warangkala tjutiningi munu kala wiyaringkunytjakutawara kala uwankara brushangka mantjilpai ka mapalku piltiringkupai munu wiyaringkupai. Ka Jennilu mantjira tjunkupai raiki panya ngayulu craftroomakutu warkaku pitjala. Ngayuku katja kulunypa kulu katipai ngali kangkurura warkaripai paintangka munu batikangka kulu.

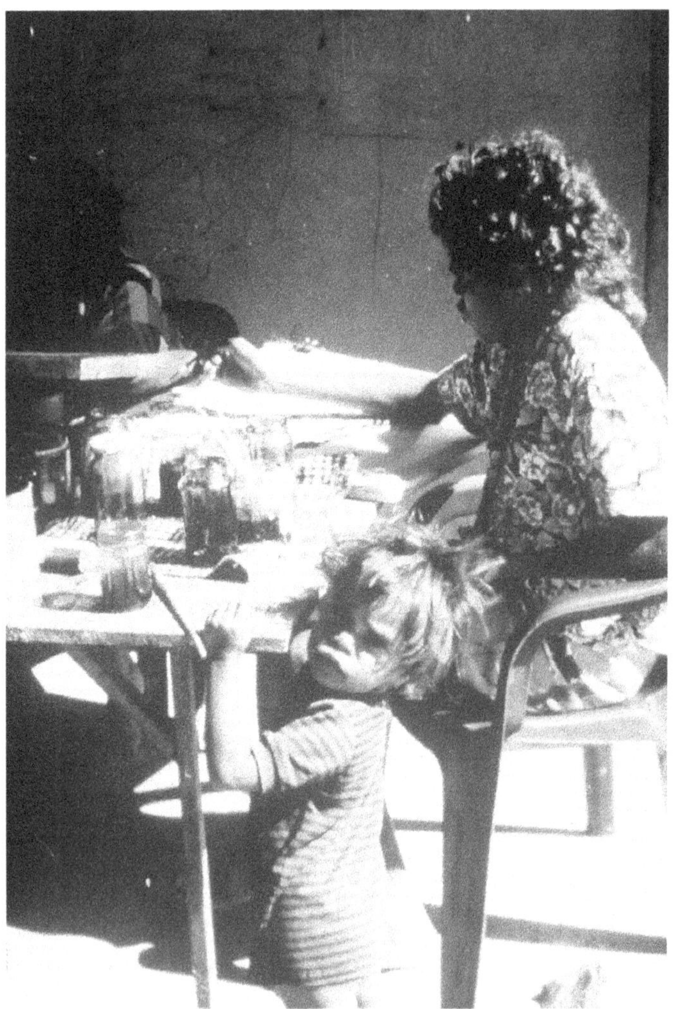

Lexie Ingkatji painting on silk, with her son Ushmer, 1995 (photograph Ute Eickelkamp)

NYUKANA BAKER
NYUKANAKU TJUKURPA

(Translation by Margaret Dagg)

I first started drawing and painting at school. After school, I came to the craftroom, right? And I worked in the craftroom, maybe painting small cards.

Win Hilliard was working in the craftroom, it used to be over there where the trees are. We came there to work – Yangkuyinya, Tjikalyinya, and me. We worked together. And Nuranya Ward. We worked in the craftroom in the afternoon, after school hours.

After I finished school, I started working in the craftroom; I didn't take any other job, like working in the clinic or in a household. I painted cards, and I made floor rugs, and – when was it? – in 1963, I went to New South Wales. For weaving. There was a workshop: weaving and tapestry. Winifred and I went together for three weeks.

In 1974, Jillian Davey, Carol's mother, and I went to Indonesia [to the batik research centre in Yogjakarta]. Winifred did not come, but a teacher, Kunmanara Finch, came with us. We flew from Alice Springs

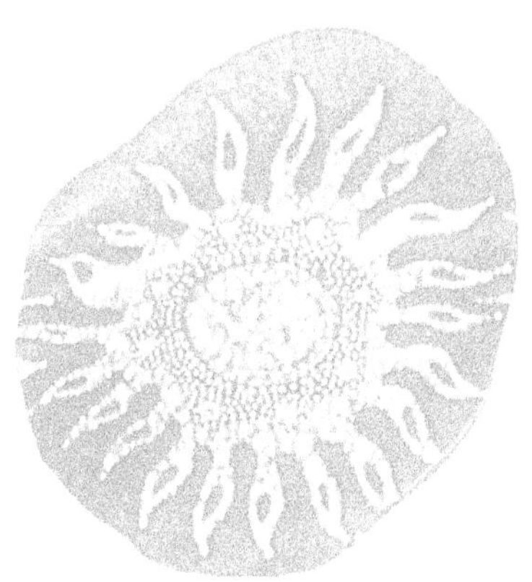

Ngayulu iriti kulangka nyinara tjitjingku walka palyalpai mununa paintamilalpai. Mununa palulanguru kula wiyaringkula ngayulu kuliningi craftroomangka warkarinytjikitjangku mununa pitjangu nyanga palula kutu munula tjinguru paintamilaningi card kulunypa tjutangka.

Ka Win Hilliardanya nyanga palula warkaringi nganmanypa craftroom nyangangka palu craftroom nganmanyitja nyarangka ngarangi nyara punu tjuta kuwari ngaranyi palula. Kala warkaku pitjapai nyara palula ngaranyangka. Munula warkarlpai Nuranya Yangkuyinya Tjikalyinya munu ngayulu nganana tjungu alatjitu warkaripai. Nganmanypala kulangka malangka pitjala nintiringkupai.

Palula malangkana kula wiyaringu mununa craftroomangka pitjala warkaringi, ngayulu warka kutjupa tjutaku mukuringkunytja wiyatu panya clinicaku munu walingka warkarinytjaku kulu palu ngayulu ngurkantanu warka nyangatja paintamilantjikitjangku munu floor rug tjuta palyantjikitjangku. Mununa 1963ngka anu New South Walesala kutu weaving nintiringkunytjikitja nyara palulana warkaku nintiringangi weavemilantjikitja munu warka kutjupa tjutaku kulu. Win Hilliardanya ngali nyara palula kutu anu munuli wiki mankurpa manyinangi nyura nyara palula.

Munu 1974ngka Jillian Daveynya Carolku ngunytju munu ngayulu anula Indonesiala kutu panya batikaku

to Darwin, but we had to go back to Ernabella because of the cyclone. There was nothing left in Darwin, no hotel, no shops. We started again and went from Sydney to Indonesia. They wanted us to stay for six weeks, but after four weeks we came back: no food in Indonesia! We only got a little bit of meat and it rained a lot. The Indonesians eat different food, no meat. Not Australian food. There was only one Australian shop, which had lots of chicken, lots of meat, and

Nyukana Baker with her daughter, Tanya Kunmanara, 1996 (photograph Ute Eickelkamp)

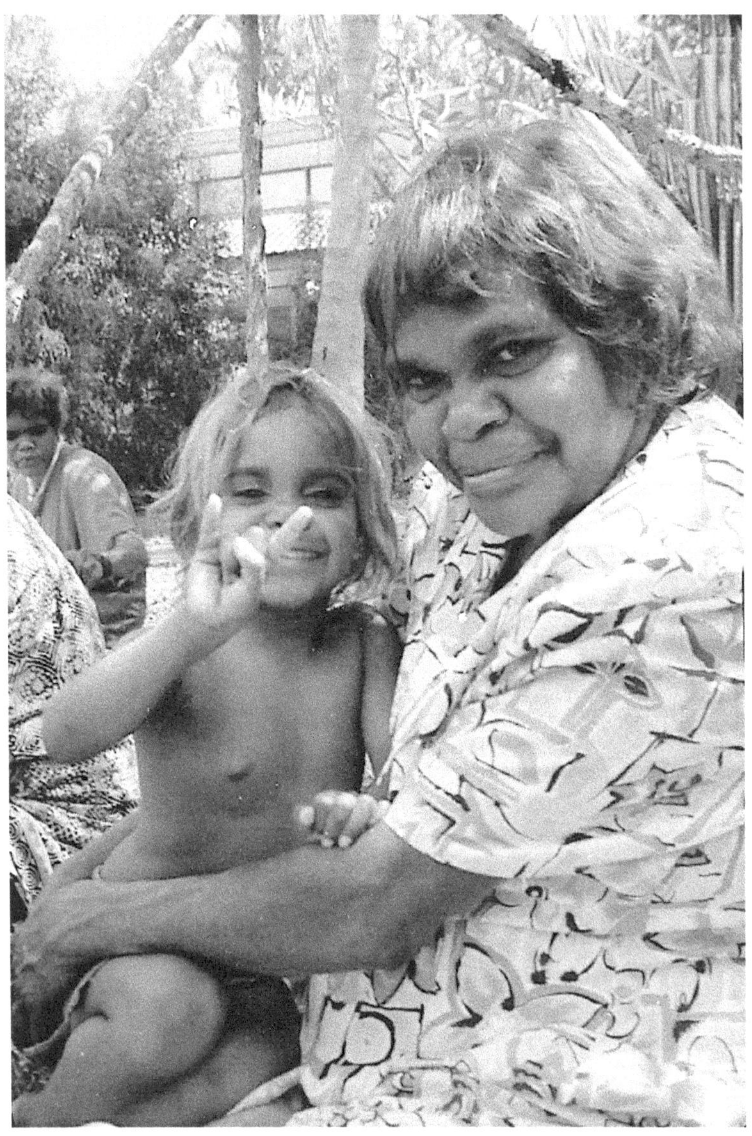

nintiringkupai ngarangi Jakartala. Ka Win Hilliardanya ngananala tjungu pitjanytja wiyatu palu kungka panya teacher pitjangu ngananala tjungu panya kunmanara Finchanya. Munula Alice Springsala nguru Darwinta kutu ma pakanu irupulaina pulkangka palu wiya nyara palula ngurula malaku pitjangu Anapalata kutu panya ngura nyara palula walpa pulka ngarangi. Ka kutjupa kutjupa ngaranytja wiya Darwinta uwankara alatjitu katantara minyaminyanu tjikilpai tjuta munu tjuwa tjuta kulu kulu. Kala ngula piruku tjataringu munula Sydneyla wanu anu Indonesiala kutu. Ka paluru tjana ngananaanya tjapinu six wiki nyinanytjaku, palu four wiki kutjula nyinara wiyaringkula pitjangu. Panya ngura nyara Indonesiala mai wiya. Kala ngura nyara palula kuka tjukutjuku kutju mantjilpai. Ka minangku kulu rawangku alatjitu puyilpai. Panya Indonesiala nyinapai tjutangkuya mai kutjupa ngalkupai, kuka wiya. Australiaku mai wiya. Ka nyara palula Australiaku tjuwa kutju ngarangi. Kuka tjutatjara munu chicken munu kuka walpayatangka kulu kulu. Ka ngayulu pulkara pukularingu kukaku.

Ka batikaku panya nintiringkupainya wali pulka alatjitu, kaya wati tjuta munu minyma tjuta kulu tjungu warkaripai nyara palula. Ka ngura nyara Indonesiala tjana raiki wara pulkangka alatjitu palyalpai warka wiru mulapa. Ka nyara palula ara ngayulu ngurpangku. Putu nguwanpa palyaningi batik putu alatjituna kuwaripatjana palyaningi.

Nyara Indonesiala, palu ngura nyara katu kuluya wati tjuta warkaripai batikakangka munuya tjatangka kulu walka tjunkupai

tin meat. I was really happy about the meat.

The batik workshop was big: many men and women took part. The Indonesian materials are huge and they make beautiful batik. At that stage, I didn't know how to make batik. I couldn't do it.

In Indonesia, but also in the top end of Australia, men work with batik, as well. They make T-shirts and screenprints. I don't know why only women work in the Ernabella craftroom.

The craftroom

In the past, many women came to the craftroom, working together like this: six women were making large floor rugs, three sitting on one side and three on the other, the floor rug in between them. One woman would make the design: she painted it on the hessian and the others hooked the wool. They made the design out of coloured wool, the outline in black on a grey or brown background. The women chose the colours themselves and they still do it that way nowadays.

Yes, the craftroom is a place for women to work. As the chairperson, I look after it: I might make sure that it's clean and I oversee the work, yes. I select works for exhibitions, have meetings, do the budget and make suggestions to the coordinator.

Nowadays, the art coordinators don't stay for too long. After maybe two years they go and we get a new one. I think that's good – a new person might have different ideas, might bring new things to learn.

Kukika is my little niece. I'm looking after her. She's already learning in the craftroom. She knows

munuya paintamilalpai ka ngayulu putu kulini nya kula panyatja minyma kutju warkaripai craftroomangka.

Craftroomatjara wangkanytja

Kuwaripatjara mulapaya minyma tjuta mulapa warkaku pitjapai craftroomakutu, munuya nyanga alatji warkaripai minyma mankurpaya kampa kutjupa nyinapai ka minyma mankurpa kutjupa kampa kutjupa nyinapai floor rug ngururpa tjunkula. Ka nganmanytju minyma kutjungku walkatjunkupai kaya palulanguru wool kalatjara tjuta katalpai munuya wakalpailta. Munuya wakara uwankara wiyara mala patilpai marungka munta tjinguru kala greyngka munta tjinguru brownta walka utiringkunytjaku. Minyma tjutangkuya walytjangku kala palunya tjananya ngurkantankupai munu tjana kuwari kulu nyanga palu purunypa palyalpai.

Panya craftroom nyanga paluru minyma tjutaku nyinara warkarinytjaku. Ka ngayulu chairperson nyinara tjananya nyakupai wirura warkarinyangka panya kuranyitjangku alatji nyakupai wirura warkarinyangka munu kilina kanyinnyangka mununa warka wiru mulapa palyantjitja nguru raiki tjutanguru ngurkantara tjunkupai exhibition kutu katinytjaku ka panya tjana utitjunkunyangka kutjupa tjutangku nyakula payamilapailta munula tjunguringkula wangkara kulira palyalpai.

Ka ara nyanga kuwaritjangka piranpa panya mayatja nyinanytjatjanu paluru rawa nyinapai wiya tjukutjuku nyinara paluru ankupai tjinguru yiya kutjara nyinanytjatjanu munuya ankupai kala kutjupa mantjilpai. Munula kulilpai nyangatja wiru tjingurulanya mayatja

a little bit. She practises on canvas and paints witchetty grubs and honeyants.

Yes, the craftroom is a good place, but it's true, there are problems outside. It was different in mission times, no petrol – that was locked away in a wooden hut, no rubbish. It was really beautiful, but nowadays – I think it's over.

Life on the mission

It used to be nice. In the morning, we were at our places, in the wiltja, and then we went and had a shower. And in the kitchen, we ate breakfast. There was plenty of meat in the kitchen, we had porridge and bread. The women made bread early in the morning and at noon.

When breakfast was over, we went to church. And after church, to school, or to work. The women would go and pick up some wool for spinning. Not the men. They had different jobs, but the old men didn't work, they sat down. It was hard for the old people: no pension money. All the young fellows were working. Those who didn't work got only a little bit of food, very little.

And all the children went to school, had lunch, and then, after school, we went out bush. The children got no supper, only breakfast and lunch. So we went out on donkeys, looking for rabbits and witchetty grubs. We

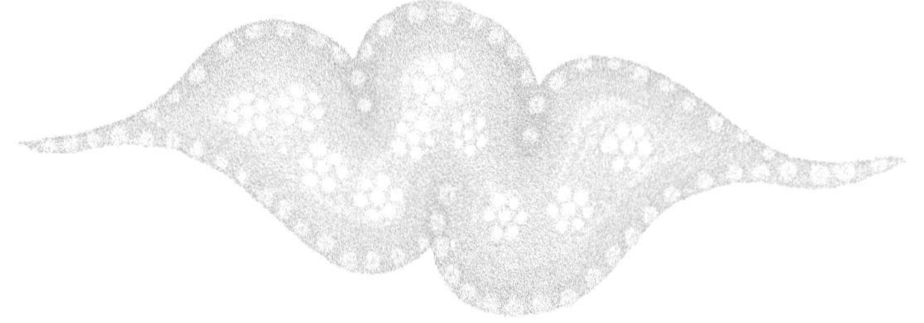

kutjupangku kulintja wirutjarangku warka wiruku kuwaritjaku nintilku.

Uwa tjitji nyanga Susannga ngayuku ukari, ka ngayulu palunya atunymankupai. Ka paluru mukuringkupai nintiringkunytjikitja munu paluru nganmanytju alatjitu walkatjura nintiringangi canvasangka paintamilara maku munu tjala paluru nganmanypa alatjitu nintiringangi paluru mukuringkula.

Uwa craftroom nyangatja wiru mulapa, palu tjukarurungkuna wangkanyi, panya kura kutjupa kutjupa tjuta urilta ngaranyitu kuwari nyanga. Palu iriti wiru mulapa ngarangi munu kutjupa alatjitu pitulu wiya kaya piranpa tjutangku tjanampa pitulu patira tjunkupai wali tjukutjukungka munu ngura kulu raputji wiya ngarangi kilina alatjitu, palu kuwari nyanga wiyaringu munu kurakura ngaranyi.

Mission dayngka nyinanytja

Uwa iriti wiru mulapa ngarangi. Kala wiltja walytjangka walytjangka nyinapai, munula mungawinki pakara ankupai showerngka paltjintjikitja. Munula palulanguru kitjinangka mai ngalkupai. Ka nyara palula kuka pulka ngaripai ngulaku palu maila ngalkupai munu paritji kulu. Kaya minyma tjutangku mai bread tjuta pitjala paulpai mungawinki mulapa munu mungartji kulu.

Kala palulanguru mai ngalkula wiyaringkula uwankara ankupai church kutu inmaku munula churchangka malangka ankupai kulakutu munta tjinguru kutjupa tjuta warkakutu. Kaya minyma tjutangku ankula wool mantjilpai rungkantjikitjangku, palu wati wiya. Tjana warka kutjupangka warkaripai. Kaya wati tjilpi tjuta

might go to Aeroplane. The girls went together. And at night-time, we slept in our wiltja. Yes, we still look for witchetty grubs today, but we don't go on donkeys anymore. And sometimes, we still camp out bush.

Yes, the old people talk about what it was like before mission times. A long time ago, there was always water running in the creek. That was truly beautiful in the old days.

Talking about art

I first learnt the Ernabella design as a schoolgirl, by telling stories in the sand – milpatjunanyi, the storytelling game.

I have always made the Ernabella design and my own design has changed only a little bit over the years, and yes, each artist has got her own design. Margaret Dagg's looks a bit like mine, that's right.

Before I draw the design with wax on the scarf, I have an idea. Yes, some people think this is spinifex, or stars, something, but wiya, it's not.

But I also make dot paintings. This is when I paint spinifex, trees, witchetty grubs. But not with the design in batik. The dot paintings were started by Tjulkiwa and Makinti in the mid-1980s. It was not brought here by other people. I had no idea how to do it, and then I learnt a little bit; I watched them.

I also travelled to Fiji and to Japan, and yes, they've got their own design. But the Ernabella design is different. It has changed over the years, and with different mediums, but yes, it's still the same. I have never wanted to paint something totally different.

Painting a walka is telling a story in your mind. Old ladies don't do it, only girls and younger women. They

warka wiya nyinapai. Ka ara nyanga paluru wituwitu mulapa ngarangi kuwaripatjara wati tjilpi tjutaku panya iritiya tjilpi tjutangku pension mani mantjilpai wiya. Yangupala tjuta kutjuya warkaripai mani mantjintjikitja. Kaya kutjupa tjutangku panya warka wiya nyinapai tjutangku mai tjukutjuku kutju mantjilpai iriti.

Kala tjitji tjuta kuulangka nyinapai munula palulanguru kula wiyaringkula pakara ngura kutu ankupai. Panya nganana supper ngalkupai wiya kitjinangka pinpatja munu dinner kutjula ngalkupai kitjinangka. Munula palulanguru ankupai donkey tjutangka tatira kuka rapitaku munu makuku kulu. Uwa Irupulainala kutula rawa ankupai munula mungaringkunyangka nganana kungka tjuta wiltjangka ngaripai. Palu nganana kuwari kulu makuku ankupai palu donkey tjutala kuwari kanyintja wiya munula putikutu ankupaitu antjaki ngarinytjikitja.

Kaya tjilpi tjutangku ara irititja rawangkutu wangkapai panya tjana ngura wirungka nyinanytjatjanungku. Ka iriti mulapa mina pulka karungka rawa ukalingkupai ka wiru mulapa ngarapai nyara palula arangka.

Warkatjara wangkanytja

Uwa ngayulu kuwaripatjara mulapa nintiringu Anapalaku walka palyantjikitja tjitji kulitja mununa milpatjunkula mantangka walka palyalpai tjukurpa wangkara.

Ngayulu rawangku Anapalaku walka palyalpai ka ngayuku panya walka kutjuparingu munu ngalya wiruringangi yiya panya nyara malakitja tjutangka palu minyma uwankarangkula walka kutjupa kutjupa katangku kanyini walytjangku

didn't do it in the old days – iriti wiya!

I also make carvings. I like small carvings: little cats, tinka and wombats.

What do you think about collecting your stories for a book?

It's a good idea to write our stories down. One day, the young people can listen to the tapes and read the book, so they can learn about our history. The children should also learn English.

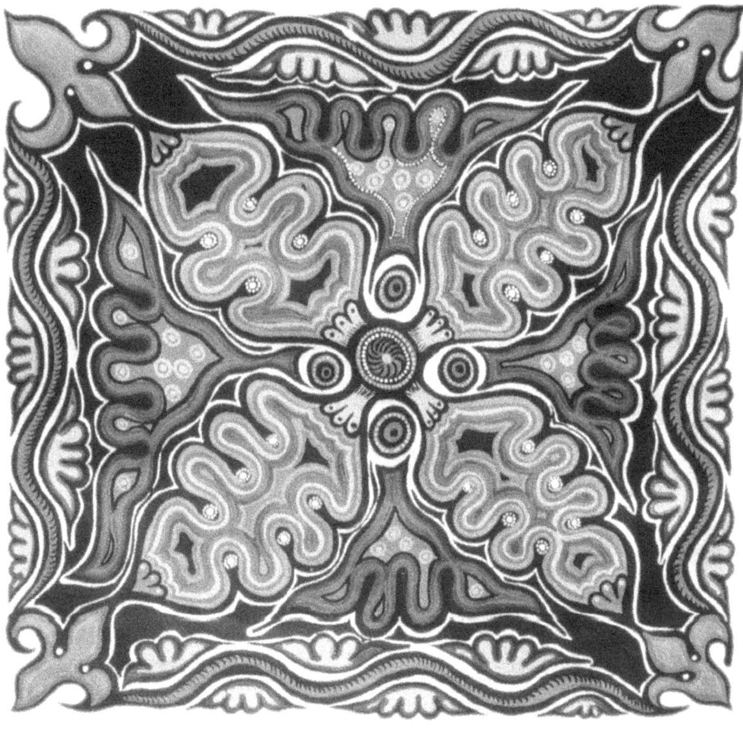

Gouache on canvas, by Alison Carroll, 1990s (Michelle Swanborough collection, photograph Ute Eickelkamp)

walytjangku, ka Margaretaku walka ngayuku purunypa.

Palu walkatjunkunytja kuwaripangkana kulilpai tjanpi munu kililpi palyannyangka palku palu wiya.

Panya dot painting nyanga palunya Tjulkiwalu walkatjunangi munu Makintilu kulu tjinguru 1980ngka. Ngayulu ngurpa nyinangi nyara palulaara mununa tjanalanguru nyakula nintiringu.

Ngayulu iriti Fijilakutu anu munu Japantakutu kulu mununa nyangu panya tjanayanku walka walytjangku palyantjantjanungku kanyini ngura nyara palula tjanala. Palu Anapalaku walka kutjupa alatjitu. Munu walka paluru kutjuparingu yiya panya nyaranta palu kutjuparinytja mulapa wiya panya walka palunyaya kutjupangka kutjupangka palyalpai. Panya ngayulu mukuringkunytja wiyatu nguratjara walkatjunkunytjikitja.

Munu ngayulu walkatjunkula tjukurpa purunypa tjakultjunanyi. Palu minyma pampa tjutangkuya walka tjunkupai wiya, kungkawara tjutangku munu minyma malatja tjutangku kutjuya palyalpai palu iritiya palyalpai wiya.

Kana ngayulu punu palyalpai tjati kulunypa tjuta munu ngintaka tjuta munu wampata tjuta langka tjuta.

Yaltjin kulini panya ngayulu tjukurpa mantjini nyiringka tjunkunytjikitjangku?

Uwa palyana kulini nyangatja wiru alatjitu nganampa tjukurpa nyiringka tjunkunytjaku. Tjinguru ngula tjitji malatja tjutangku tapeanguru kulira ritamilanma. Munu tjana nyara palulanguru nganampa tjukurku nintiringkuku munu tjana uti ingkilitjaku kulu nintiringama.

ALISON CARROLL
ALISONAKU TJUKURPA

(Translation by Kanytjupai Armstrong)

I come from Ernabella, but for most of my school years I was in Alice Springs, staying at St Philips College. I came back to Ernabella for a short while after I had finished high school. Then I went to Alice Springs again, to Yirara College.

Back in Ernabella, I started working in the craftroom, only for a little while, maybe one or two years. Win Hilliard, that old lady, was the coordinator. At that time, I painted Ernabella design on bookmarks and cards, and I also made batik. I first learnt about walka as a schoolgirl. After school, we went and watched the women working in the craftroom.

Then I decided to become a health worker and I worked at the clinic for many years. I would still go to the craftroom sometimes. During holidays, I went to my aunty's homeland, Youngs Well.

My mother used to work in the craftroom. She did batik, weaving and painting. She taught me a lot. As schoolchildren we would come and watch the older women working on batiks. They let us try a little – this is how we learnt. The craftroom is a good place for young girls. They come here after school with their teachers; they also visit other places to have a look: EV/TV [Ernabella Video/Television], or the community office.

Nowadays, I come to the craftroom every day. I mainly do batik and sometimes silk painting, or gouache on canvas.

I have never tried to paint anything else, only Ernabella design. This is what we have always painted.

Ngayuluna Anapalalanguru palu ngayulu rawa nyinangi schoolangka yiya tjuta Alice Springsala ngura panya St Philip Collegeala mununa malaku pitjapai unytju munu tjukutjuku nyinara malaku ankupai mununa high school wiyaringkula piruku Yirara Collegeala nyinangi.

Palulanguruna malaku Anapalaku pitjala warkaringi craftroomangka unytju nguwanpana warkaringi tjinguru yiya kutju munta kutjara. Win Hilliardanya minyma piranpa panyatja nganampa mayatja ka nyara palula ara ngayulu paintamilalpai Anapalaku walka nyiri pulkangka munu nyiri tjukutjukungka mununa batikangka kulu warkaringi. Walka nyanga palumpara nintiringu tjitjilpi schoolangka mununa schoolangka malangka ankupai craftroomakutu. Minyma tjutangku palyannyangka nyakunytjikitja.

Palulanguruna ngayulu mukuringu healthworker warkarinytjikitja

Alison Carroll painting on silk, 1995 (photograph Ute Eickelkamp)

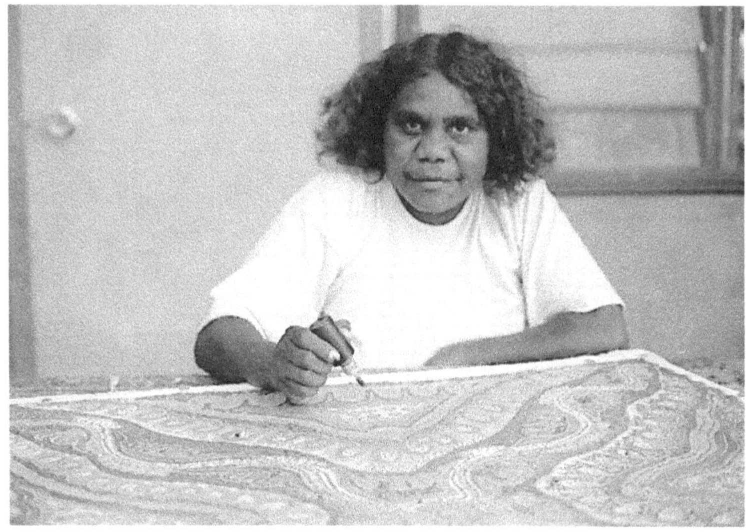

clinic-angka mununa yiya tjuta warkaringi. Mununa kutjupa ara ankupai craftroomakutu holidayangka mununa ngayuku ngunytju malatjaku ngurakutu ankupai Youngs Wellalakutu panya.

Ngayuku ngunytju craftroomangka warkaripai munu paluru batika palyalpai weavimilalpai munu paintamilalpai paluruni nintinu warka tjutaku. Ngangana schoolanguru pitjala nyakupai minyma tjutangku batik palyannyangka kalanya ungkupai arkara palyantjaku kala palyara tjukutjuku nintiringangi nyanga alatjila nintiringangi.

Craftroom nyangatja warka wiru kungkawara tjukutjuku tjuta nintiringkunytjaku. Panya tjananya teacher tjutangku katipai schoolangka malangka EV/TV kulu nyakunytjaku munu office-angka kulu nintiringkunytjaku.

Kuwari ngayulu rawa pitjapai craftroomakutu panya ngayulu palyalpai batik mununa kutjupa ara silk paintamilalpai munu canvasakulu.

Walka kutjupana paintamilantja wiyatu panya Anapalaku walka kutjuna walkatjunkupai nyanga palunya kutjula palyalpai rawangku.

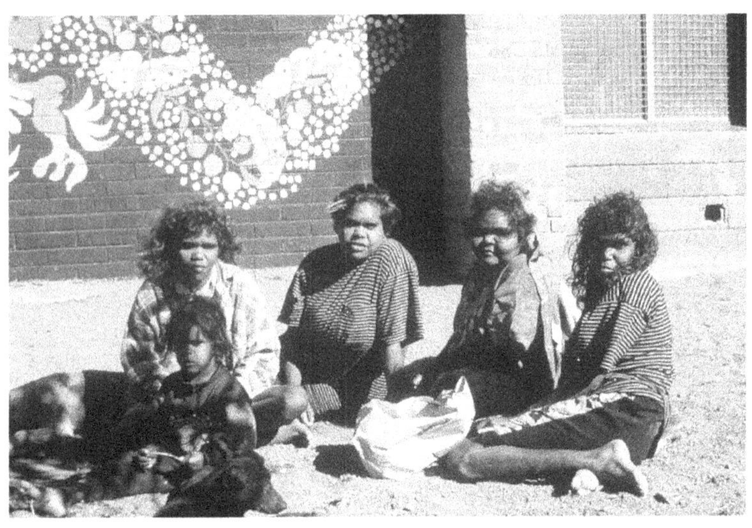

A group of young artists (left to right), Lexie Ingkatji with son Ushmer, Carol Williams, Nyuwara Tapaya, Yilpi Marks, 1996 (photograph Ute Eickelkamp)

'Pakuwiyaringkunytja . . .'

'It's time for a rest now . . .'

glossary of terms

Most of the explanatory translations are from Cliff Goddard (compiler), *Pitjantjatjara/Yankunytjatjara to English Dictionary*, second edition, Institute for Aboriginal Development, 1992.

Anangu	literally 'person', now used to refer to Aboriginal Australians in general or to indigenous speakers of Western Desert dialects
ili	fig
iriti	long ago
kalaya	emu *(Dromaius novaehollandiae)*
kaltu kaltu	edible native millet *(Panicum decompositum)*
kami	grandmother, granddaughter, grandaunt, grandniece
kampurarpa	desert raisin *(Solanum centrale)*
kuka	game, meat
kunakanti	type of grass *(Brachiaria miliiformis)*
kungka(wara)	female, teenage girl, young woman
kunmanara	substitute name to avoid using a deceased person's name or a word of similar sound
kutjara	two
mai	food from plants (flour, bread, vegetables)
maku	edible caterpillar
malu	red kangaroo *(Macropus rufus)*
mangata	quandong *(Santalum acuminatum)* (Yankunytjatjara term)
mara	hands
milpatjunanyi	literally 'putting the stick down', girls' storytelling game involving making marks in the sand to depict places and/or using leaves to represent people, accompanied by the rhythmic beating of a bent stick or piece of wire

minyma	mature woman with at least two children
miru	spearthrower with cutting edge; a multipurpose tool
ngintaka	Perentie lizard *(Varanus giganteus)*
nyalpi	leaf
ninti	familiar, known, competent, knowledgeable
pika	sick
pulka	big, large, a lot of, heavy, strong, senior person
punu	tree, wood, woodcarving
tarka	bone, stalk, bony, skinny
tinka	Gould's goanna *(Varanus gouldii)*
tjala	honeyant
tjamu	grandfather, grandson, greatuncle, greatnephew
tjitji	child
Tjukurpa	Law, Dreaming, story (tjukurpa)
tjuta	more than three, plural marker
uwa	yes
wakati	inland pigweed *(Portulaca oleracea)*
walka	meaningful mark, design, writing, natural and created patterns
walkatjunanyi	literally 'putting a mark down', to write, to draw or paint, girls' sand storytelling game with hand-drawn images only
wangunu	naked woollybutt *(Eragrostis eriopoda)*
wati	initiated man, husband, non-Aboriginal man
wayanu	quandong *(Santalum acuminatum)*
wiltja	bush hut, shade, shadow
wira	small cup-like digging scoop
wirinywirinypa	bush-tomato *(Solanum cleistogamum)* with yellow sweet fruit
wiru	nice, beautiful, lovely
wiya	no, nothing, none, not, without
yuu	windbreak, natural shelter from wind

www.ingramcontent.com/pod-product-compliance
Lightning Source LLC
LaVergne TN
LVHW060620110826
845147LV00019B/1057

* 9 7 8 0 8 5 5 7 5 3 1 0 8 *